PROBATION AND PRIVATISATION

Privatisation was introduced into the probation service on the 1st June 2014 whereby work with medium and low risk offenders went to a number of private and voluntary bodies, work with high risk offenders remained with the State. The National Probation Service (NPS) covered State work whilst the 35 existing Probation Trusts were replaced by 21 Community Rehabilitation Companies (CRCs). Staff were allocated to either side of the divide but all remained as probation officers. The effect was that the existing probation service lost control of all but 30,000 of the most high risk cases, with the other 220,000 low to medium risk offenders being farmed out to private firms. Privatisation was justified as the only available way of achieving important policy objectives of extending post release supervision to offenders on short sentences, a group who are the most prolific offenders with high reconviction rates yet who receive no statutory support.

This book describes the process by which the probation service became privatised, assessing its impact on the probation service itself, and on the criminal justice system generally. It considers both the justifications for privatisation, as well as the criticisms of it, and asks to what extent the probation service can survive such changes, and what future it has as a service dedicated to the welfare of offenders. It demonstrates how the privatisation of probation can be seen as a trend away from traditional public service in criminal justice towards an emphasis on efficiency and cost effectiveness.

This book is essential reading for criminology students engaged with criminal justice, social policy, probation, punishment and working with offenders. It will also be key reading for practitioners and policy makers in jurisdictions where there is an interest in extending their own privatisation practice.

Philip Bean is Emeritus Professor of Criminology and Criminal Justice at the University of Loughborough, UK.

PROBATION AND PRIVATISATION

Philip Bean

LONDON AND NEW YORK

First published 2019
by Routledge
2 Park Square, Milton Park, Abingdon, Oxon OX14 4RN

and by Routledge
711 Third Avenue, New York, NY 10017

Routledge is an imprint of the Taylor & Francis Group, an informa business

© 2019 Philip Bean

The right of Philip Bean to be identified as author of this work has been asserted by him in accordance with sections 77 and 78 of the Copyright, Designs and Patents Act 1988.

All rights reserved. No part of this book may be reprinted or reproduced or utilised in any form or by any electronic, mechanical, or other means, now known or hereafter invented, including photocopying and recording, or in any information storage or retrieval system, without permission in writing from the publishers.

Trademark notice: Product or corporate names may be trademarks or registered trademarks, and are used only for identification and explanation without intent to infringe.

British Library Cataloguing in Publication Data
A catalogue record for this book is available from the British Library

Library of Congress Cataloging in Publication Data
Names: Bean, Philip, 1936- author.
Title: Probation and privatisation / Philip Bean.
Other titles: Probation and privatization
Description: Abingdon, Oxon ; New York, NY : Routledge,
[2018] | Includes bibliographical references and index.
Identifiers: LCCN 2018020301| ISBN 9780815353973 (hardback)
 | ISBN 9780815353980 (pbk.) | ISBN 9781351134514 (ebook)
Subjects: LCSH: Probation–Great Britain. | Corrections–
Contracting out–Great Britain. | Privatization–Great Britain.
Classification: LCC HV9345.A5 B43 2018 | DDC 364.6/30941–dc23
LC record available at https://lccn.loc.gov/2018020301

ISBN: 978-0-8153-5397-3 (hbk)
ISBN: 978-0-8153-5398-0 (pbk)
ISBN: 978-1-351-13451-4 (ebk)

Typeset in Bembo
by Taylor & Francis Books

CONTENTS

Preface		*vii*
1	Introduction: Privatisation and neo liberalism	1
2	Government intervention	24
3	The Probation Service's response	66
4	Privatisation at work: Separate services, opening up the market and Payment by Results	87
5	Privatisation at work: "Through The Gate" and the Probation Institute	126
6	The future of probation	143

Appendices   *180*
Appendix 1: Prime Ministers from 1990 to 2018   *181*
Appendix 2: Home Secretaries from November 1990 to July 2016   *182*
Bibliography   *183*
Index   *192*

PREFACE

As an ex probation officer, albeit in those far off days of the 1960s and during the so called "Golden Age," I have become greatly concerned about the position in which the Probation Service now finds itself. What does it mean for the service to be privatised, and does it have a future, except as a divided service half of which is privatised and the other half as having reduced duties? The more I looked the more complicated the whole matter seemed to be, with accusations and counter accusations being the order of the day. It was soon clear that my memories of the probation service and my attachment to it were firmly rooted in that period when "advise, assist and befriend" was the mantra under which we lived and breathed. This is now no longer appropriate, although numerous comments in the literature suggests a number of Probation Officers are still attached to that. Even so, few would expect to return to those halcyon days when the Probation Service could do no wrong. Things have moved on since then, and even before privatisation there was a different mood and a different ethos surrounding probation and probation practice. Nonetheless privatisation, when it came, was a shock which required massive adjustments, and produced for many a belief that the service would never recover. My own view is more optimistic; it is that whatever the current position there is now an opportunity to debate and discuss what sort of probation service we might want and how best to bring it about? It is the best opportunity for decades to bring about a new service and shape it accordingly. Simply lamenting the current position will lead us nowhere.

It is customary and entirely appropriate to thank those who have given up their valuable time to discuss with me the various features of the probation service as it now exists. Accordingly, I would like to thank the following, some of whom read drafts of chapters, all of whom were prepared to spend time discussing and tolerating my endless questions. They are John Budd, Lol Burke, Peter Dawson, David Faulkner, Leo Goodman, Martin Graham, Rt. Hon. Chris Grayling, John Harding, Tony Knivett, Ian Lawrence, Rod Morgan, Robin Osmond, John Perry, Lord Ramsbotham, Dame Glenys Stacey, Sir John Weston, and Nigel Whiskin. Others too numerous to mention including friends and family played their part, for which I offer my thanks.

It is with some dismay that no one was prepared to speak with me from the National Probation Service, Community Rehabilitation Companies, and HM Prison and Probation Service. They gave no reason, simply that (where they replied, and some did not) they were not prepared to meet with me. The result, sadly, is a less than adequate account of the situation than it might have been.

Philip Bean
July 2018

1

INTRODUCTION

Privatisation and neo liberalism

In 1958, a distinguished British criminologist described the Probation Service as "the most significant contribution made by this country (the UK) to penalogical theory and practice of the 20th Century." He also thought it would most likely endure.[1] Yet some 50 years later, stripped of many of its earlier duties, divided between public and private sectors, with morale at an all-time low, and in part merged with a larger more powerful Prison Service, there appears little to support those earlier claims. To many observers the once admired Probation Service is now nothing more than a hollowed out relic of its former past.

The impact on this service and beyond has been extensive, creating change without parallel in modern criminal justice systems. Simply on the basis of the numbers of offenders under its control the loss has been immense. On the 1st June 2014, when it was privatised, the Probation Service lost all but 30,000 of the most high risk cases, with the other 220,000 low to medium risk offenders allocated to private companies. Two of those companies, Interserve and Sodexo took over more than half what was once the remit of the Probation Service.

Does it matter that the service has changed so much? At one level probably not; it was always a small service in terms of the numbers of its staff, compared with that of the Prison Service or the Police. The number of offenders on probation was also small, compared to those dealt with by the Police – although it dealt with three times more offenders than were in prison. Yet the Probation Service from its inception always appeared to have a weighty influence on the criminal justice system. In its modern form the 1948 Criminal Justice Act provided it with additional basic legal requirements and firmly established it as a criminal justice agency. From that it developed into a flourishing service, which around the late 1960s and early 1970s, in what could be called its Golden Age,[2] it was feted by governments, approved by all and sundry, and seemed unstoppable in its meteoric rise. At one point it was referred to as "the jewel in the penal system." Yet if not quite the jewel, or even the centre of the penal system, it certainly had unprecedented acclaim.

Introduction to the privatisation debate

The main reason given by the Coalition Government for privatising the Probation Service, according to the House of Commons Justice Committee's Report was to "extend support to short sentenced prisoners," and doing so by "facilitating innovation through the involvement of the private and voluntary sector providers in rehabilitative provisions." As part of this aim the government wanted "to introduce services for the most prolific offenders thereby rectifying a long standing anomaly ... whereby those who tend to be the most prolific offenders receive no statutory support."[3] That long standing anomaly was the high reconviction rate of those sentenced to 12 months imprisonment or less, and the lack of provision and services for this group on release. The question was how best to achieve this and do so by providing better value for the taxpayer? The government's solution, according to Andrew Selous, Parliamentary Secretary of State for Justice, was to bring in the best of the public voluntary sector and the private sector to work with offenders to reduce offending rates.[4] It would do so by being more efficient, more effective, and more economical. It was recognised that this approach carried a risk, in that it may not work, but the government's response was there was a greater risk in leaving things as they are. The risk in doing nothing would mean continuing with high rates of reoffending, leaving short sentenced offenders without support on release.

The path chosen by the government, therefore, was to address a long standing problem. It did not need to go down the privatisation route, it could have chosen a different path. There were alternatives. Nonetheless, it chose to go a certain way, and in so doing produced a solution which remains highly contentious. The plans for reforming the Probation Service were set out in a White Paper in 2013 entitled *Transforming Rehabilitation* [5] and were implemented under the Offender Rehabilitation Act 2014.[6] The aspirational aims were to open up the market to a diverse range of providers, and to introduce new payment incentives to be directed towards a real reduction in offending.

There were four specific objectives. First, to split the community services between the National Probation Service (the NPS) and the private sector, the Community Rehabilitation Companies (the CRCs). The NPS was to be responsible for high risk offenders and the CRCs for the medium and low risk group. This meant the NPS remained as before within the control of the public sector. The CRCs were to be in the private and voluntary sector, and operate under contracts.

The second and third objectives were to produce a joined-up rehabilitation service across prisons and the community. This would mainly involve the CRCs. Mandatory supervision was to be imposed on all who were serving a prison sentence of 12 months or less. This would eventually involve many thousands of offenders who had hitherto received no supervision on discharge and no formal attempts at rehabilitation.

The fourth objective was to provide incentives for reducing reoffending using a system of Payment by Results (PbR). The Green Paper *Breaking the cycle* said "We will pioneer a world first, – a system where we only pay for results delivered by a diverse range of providers from all sectors."[7] PbR is complicated, involving payments based on assumptions about workloads and reoffending. This is dealt with in more detail in later chapters, at this stage I only want to point out that PbR was central to the government's privatisation programme.

Unsurprisingly, these changes have produced massive disruption to the Probation Service generally, and proved unwanted to most Probation Officers. Objections came from various quarters, and in various forms; some about the imposition of the private sector on a public service, others more specific about the workings of the Probation

Service and the likely impact on thee offenders. A brief description of the service, noting some of its key features of some of the principles and precepts about what it traditionally stood for will perhaps help explain some of the criticisms levelled against privatisation, and its reaction to those criticisms.

Some features of the Probation Service, early, and late

It is difficult, if not impossible, to define and describe the major characteristics of a service which has operated for more than 150 years: the best that can be done is highlight some of its major features. So, at its peak – around the late 1960s early 1970s – the service had an extensive range of duties. It prepared Reports for all the courts, civil as well as criminal, and at all levels. It supervised juvenile and adult offenders alike, including those on licence from Detention Centres and Borstal, on Young Prison Licence, as well as supervising licensed adult prisoners including those on parole. It was also involved in what was called "kindred social work," a rather amorphous term meaning almost anything that came the Probation Service's way, including "matrimonial reconciliation." This in contrast to the immediate period before privatisation when it had fewer duties, and the post privatisation period when it had even fewer.

Even so, it was still an active service right up to the time it was privatised. To give some idea of the extent of its work these are the figures for the year 2011, i.e. three years before privatisation. Then the caseload was 243,000, and of these 160,000 offenders were on court orders, the remainder were on post release supervision. The average length of a Community Order for offenders was 14.9 months, where 55% of these orders ran their course and were completed successfully, with another 10% terminated for "good progress." The remainder were either breached for failing to comply with the conditions of their order or the offenders were convicted of a further offence. The figures show that 32% of those on an order had seven or more previous convictions, suggesting the service was often dealing with serious offenders, although there were equally many who were less serious. The service prepared 218,000 reports for the courts.[8]

The service has traditionally supervised a whole range of offenders, many with long standing personal problems, and many with the characteristics we associate with disadvantage. For example, in 2001, 66% of the men and 55% of the women being supervised had problems of drug use, and 52% of the men and 71% of the women had no qualifications from school or work. There were 67% who were unemployed, and 48% had literacy levels of 11years or below, with 14% of the women and 7% of the men being classed as psychotic.[9] These figures suggest the service was dealing with some of the more difficult offenders to rehabilitate.

During most of its history, and especially during that Golden Age, there were numerous characteristics which distinguished the Probation Service from other criminal justice agencies. Traditionally the service offered a vision of a penal system where crime was as a result of defects in personal relationships, created as a result of a malign influence on offender's lives. This was in contrast to that vision which involved just deserts and deterrence. That Probation vision or "the probation ideal," as it was often called was the centrepiece through which the probation image was kept alive.

Protecting this ideal was important. It was more than concern about resisting change but about protecting an ethos, an approach, an ideology, an aura perhaps. For a service that seldom sought publicity it had nonetheless acquired a certain mystique. It was able to paint pictures according to its own precepts and images. Its training and expertise always emphasised the plight of the offender, often pointing to defects in the offender's background or upbringing as the basis of that plight. As such it was a strong supporter of the type of rehabilitation which was based on developing a personal relationship between the Probation Officer and the offender. The strength of that relationship would supposedly determine the outcome; a strong relationship would mean an increase in personal welfare and perhaps less criminality, the converse leading to more. Personal relationships therefore were the key. Those relationships were not only aimed at directing the offender towards a better future, but to offset the detriments and failings of the offender's past. Rehabilitation, according to the Probation Service, was best achieved through human contact. In this it claimed to excel.

There is little doubt the Probation Service was strengthened and advanced by the reputation gained for the honesty and probity of its officers which stemmed from their background and their sense of public commitment. Generally speaking, the service has been trusted by the courts and the public alike – and indeed by almost all the offenders with whom it has been in contact. What has always been demanded of its officers was a certain type of person – almost saint like according to some commentators – with a strong focus towards public service. And in this respect it appears to have been successful, whether in the creation of its image, or the actions of its staff. An ethic of public service was often underpinned by a religious or political belief, and frequently a mixture of both. The book *The golden age of probation* (2014), written by a number of officers recalling their career experiences, is instructive on this point. Many became successful and did so from relatively humble origins, but were attracted to probation work by a deep sense of Christian belief and charity. The public service ethic was their driving force and was freely acknowledged and accepted. It had to be, for they were certainly not well paid. Jim Cannings, who later became Chief Probation Officer in Derbyshire said when working in London in the 1960s he was not "earning enough to keep a family" and "less than some of the young men on probation working as scaffolders or digging tunnels on extensions to the Underground."[10] And this after a three year training programme, two of which were at university and one on a poorly paid Home Office grant.

I do not want to convey an image of Probation Officers as always being wrapped around a saintly do-good image, unable to change with the times and unaffected by the outside world. That was never true of all Probation Officers and at all times. And certainly less so after the mid 1970s and beyond. Nonetheless the saintly approach still lingered although it was gradually replaced, at least in some quarters, and sometimes very slowly, by a new group of officers wanting to know what works and how best to reduce criminality. These later Probation Officers were no less hard working than their predecessors, but for the most part were more willing to move away from a casework-therapeutic approach, being otherwise trained and more knowledgeable about crime and offenders. In the mid 1970s for example the problem of substance abuse was taken more seriously, and closer alliances were being made with the voluntary sector. Drug workers were coming into the offices to carry out joint assessments in ways that never occurred before.

Times were changing, but whether the change was as comprehensive or as swift as required is a moot point.

Nor do I wish to convey the image of a service in its "Golden Age" staffed by high quality Probation Officers, who, when compared with the post privatised officers, were superior in every way. It is easy to believe the "Golden Age" was the high point of probation practice, and the service has deteriorated thereafter, but things were never that simple. Had there been such inspections during that "Golden Age" as there are in the post privatised world I suspect some awkward truths would have been revealed. Not all officers were hard working, skilful, and beloved by their "clients." Such faults as existed were never brought out into the open, inadequacies were covered by keeping out of the spotlight.

Yet in spite of it all, most governments, at least since the 1990s, did see the Probation Service as a dedicated service, although they may not have seen it as an organisation that fitted easily into the modern criminal justice system. It was an awkward service administratively. It was not part of the custodial system, its members generally being unsympathetic to the prison system, yet it was required to supervise offenders on release. Nor was it part of the community system, members also seemingly unsympathetic to the Community Service Order which they regarded as punitive, albeit that community service provided an alternative to custody. And the Probation Order itself was odd, in that it was a Court Order yet was "instead of punishment," i.e. not a community penalty in the strictest legal sense of that term. The offender had to agree to being placed on probation, a legal anomaly if there ever was one. In short it seemed not to belong anywhere.

Its connection and relationship to the courts, and its subsequent rise to prominence, can only be understood in terms of the history of the service. Briefly, this goes back at least to the mid-19th Century when famously John Augustus, a cobbler from Boston, Massachusetts, USA, undertook to stand bail for offenders and supervise them before their sentence. He was not an officer of the court, this was a later development, but he did offer a service which the courts accepted. He was apparently successful, especially dealing with offenders with alcohol problems and those who were poor. So much so that his approach and techniques were taken up by a number of others who continued the work. The basis of probation was therefore settled early; instead of a sentence of the court the offender was looked after for a stipulated period by a person who cared for the offender's welfare. It was rehabilitation or reform was based on a belief in the welfare of the offender. The court became the Probation Officer's power base.

From these rather humble beginnings the Probation Service flourished and for the latter half of the 20th Century was prominent in criminal justice. It became an internationally respected service, as well as a national one. The change therefore from that somewhat lofty position to that following privatisation has been unprecedented, whether so compared with any other government department, but let alone in criminal justice. It is doubtful if much of that early ethos has remained, there being few remnants of that original probation ideal. Privatisation has changed that, and in ways that are likely to be permanent. Was this the correct way forward? Was it right to make such unprecedented changes? The debate continues. For some, such as Francis Maude, a Cabinet Office Minister, there was a belief that privatisation offered a future where the Probation Service should challenge traditional public service structures and unleash the pent-up ideas and innovation that has been stifled by bureaucracy (November 2010). For others such as the Magistrates Association there was more doubt. It said there was no evidence that anything that was proposed would work.

The optimism of Francis Maude is striking compared with the pessimism of others, including the Magistrates Association. Yet these differences are replicated in much of the later debate; on the one hand privatisation is to be welcomed, on the other to be doubted and occasionally reviled. Parts of the debate are definitional – about what is meant by "privatisation" – it being a term which can have pejorative overtones especially when used by some political commentators. More often the debate is about the impact of privatisation on a public service and the justification for introducing the private sector into a public service, especially when related to a wider paradigm of what is called neo liberalism.

The neo liberal ideal and privatisation

Privatisation operates within a wider geo-political framework which has dominated government thinking since the early 1970s. That is best described as the neo liberal ideal. The neo liberal ideal is a generic concept where the dominant features are the "greater use of private sector providers" and "contestability," or competition which is introduced into the public sector from the private sector. Implicit are other aims: that the public sector be properly managed, and provide value for money. Underpinning this neo liberal ideal are numerous value systems one of which is a "popular punitive culture," another is the belief that the private sector is more effective and efficient than the public sector, and that the private sector is more innovative and adaptable to change. Taken together these make up the central tenets of neo liberalism, a paradigm which has dominated criminal justice generally, and the Probation Service in particular for the last four decades.

Examples of the neo liberal ideal are found throughout government, wherever there is the mixture of political intent and the economic demands of effectiveness. Take for example that from the Labour Party's manifesto in 1997 which famously said it would be "tough on crime, tough on the causes of crime." Similarly, 13 years later, in 2010, in a Ministry of Justice Green Paper that same government announced that "Significant amounts of public money have been spent on rehabilitating criminals without holding services to account for the results they achieve. We will move to a new approach where providers are increasingly paid by their results at reducing reoffending."[11]

Neo liberalism is bound up with the political, economic, and social arrangements within society that emphasise market relations, retasking the role of the state, and individual responsibility. More directly, and for these purposes, it is about providing a more effective, efficient, and economically improved public service. As such it rubs awkwardly against a service, such as the Probation Service, which has traditionally not been concerned with promoting effective and efficient ways of working. To a large extent this book is about the clash between these traditional probation values and those of modern neo liberalism, with the consequential success of the latter. It is about a movement which began when the Probation Service was just past its height, and has continued to the present day where the service has been deprived of most of its traditional practices. It is essentially about a conflict model in criminal justice where the government has imposed its demands on an unwilling public sector institution. Neo liberalism is about introducing the private sector into the public service, improving levels of management, and introducing ideas into the public sector which were never seen before. It is about challenging that more traditional world view which was taken for granted by many of those involved in probation practice, and which came as a shock when those traditional values were successfully challenged. It is also about asking the question as to whether neo liberalism in its more trenchant form was appropriate to a service as vulnerable to change as was the Probation Service.

Privatisation is but one component of the neo liberal ideal. There are others; managerialism is one, although this is often merged into privatisation but it can remain separate and be a feature in its own right. Marketisation is another.[12] They all share a common approach – to introduce private sector practices into the public sector. Moreover they all bring into the debate the assertion that the public sector will benefit from private sector initiatives, and in so doing provide additional benefits to all concerned.

Privatisation has been justified in numerous ways. Aside from any direct political considerations (such as an attack on trade union power), it was part of the Private Finance Initiative (PFI) which was used first in public works such as schools, prisons, and infrastructure. It was introduced to the railways primarily to increase capital investment, to the Post Office to increase efficiency, and into the Probation Service to increase competitiveness. The opposite to privatisation is of course nationalisation, where it is interesting that this has been introduced for the same reasons as has privatisation; for example the London Underground was nationalised in the 1920s to increase efficiency, as the private sector running the Underground was said to be inefficient. These opposites are not always mirror images. Political considerations distort the picture, as with say, the nationalisation of the steel industry, which was aimed at "controlling the command the heights of the economy." There is nothing quite like this with privatisation, although some supporters of privatisation take an equally distinct political view. Moreover, privatisation and nationalisation are rarely single issue exercises, although the dominating themes seem to be removing unnecessary costs to the taxpayer and improving the efficiency of services. In Australia, for example, such projects as the Gateway Bridge, the Logan Toll Road, and the sale of the Fish Board were all aimed at making them more efficient.[13]

For most of the 19th Century and parts of the 20th Century most criminal justice services were under private companies. In the 19th Century prisons and madhouses were part of the private sector, and the early history of probation had a similar input, financially and morally, as other private sector enterprises. The criminal justice system as a bulwark of public service is therefore a relatively new phenomena. In this sense one could see the modern version of privatisation in criminal justice as not so much a new development, more as a way of returning criminal justice to its earlier historic roots.

Privatisation is a term often used to include any form by which the government intervenes in the private sector. It is often used interchangeably with "outsourcing." As used here I want to be rather more specific and talk of privatisation as occurring when the whole or part of the public sector has its business and its assets transferred to a commercial company. That commercial company will not be accountable to the public, Parliament, or its ministers, but to its shareholders. If the whole of the assets are transferred this can be called "full" privatisation in which case the company takes over lock, stock, and barrel all the assets, as with the privatisation of some water companies or electricity companies. Even so, these companies often work to regulators (OFWAT for example) who determine such matters as pricing, service standards etc. Whether so or not, we can say that full privatisation occurs when all profits go to shareholders. Also, in "full" privatisation the company raises its own capital and income streams, and uses them to finance whatever it chooses to undertake. It is more or less free of interference from government, that is, apart from whatever regulatory framework is imposed by legislation. If only a section of the assets are transferred this still falls within the remit of privatisation, as defined here, albeit that it comes in less than the full version.

Privatisation differs from outsourcing. Whereas privatisation occurs when the private company owns the assets, outsourcing occurs when private companies sell their products to the private sector in the same way as they sell their products elsewhere. Generally speaking there are two types of outsourcing. The first is where a government agency such as the Probation Service is required to purchase the product, and the second type is where that government agency has a choice about whether it wishes to purchase. We can link privatisation and outsourcing by placing privatisation on the top of a scale, called Level 1, and outsourcing on Levels 2 and 3. An example of Level 2 would be where a private company, sells "tags" to be placed on offenders, and the product, "tagging," is purchased by a government agency such as the Probation Service, which uses them as part of its legislative duties. An example of Level 3 would be where the Probation Service purchases, say, drug testing equipment, or drug programmes from a private contractor, and may or may not operate these themselves. All three of these Levels occur here, although we shall be concerned mainly with Level 1.

Inevitably there are different types of Level 1 privatisation, some less "full" than others, but all fall within this general definition. The government may regulate the enterprise through legislation and through contracts or franchises, or, it may hold the assets and make them available on certain conditions, or simply pay for the service through the PFI. Or in some circumstances, it may allow a private company to manage the buildings or other assets and employ the staff, as in the case of private prisons.[14] All of these come within the definition of privatisation.

The form of privatisation used in the Probation Service is slightly different from that used elsewhere, and has some unusual features. Part of the Probation Service remains within the public sector, i.e. the National Probation Service (NPS), while the other was transferred to the CRCs, and it is this that was privatised. The NPS has remained in the control of government as before. In the CRCs the ownership of assets was fully transferred, with staff employed by the CRCs and according to TUPE regulations. (TUPE is the Transfer of Undertakings (Protection of Employment)). These regulations apply when a business changes owner and gives the employees legal protection. Transfers which go from the public to the private sector are not usually covered by TUPE, but they have been applied in this case.) CRCs are within the compass of privatisation, with their assets and profits now belonging to its shareholders.

However, there are some rather messy arrangements in this privatisation programme. For example, the NPS and the CRCs still share the same offices, which complicates ownership of assets. Also, the contracts for the CRCs are based on some rather curious requirements, such as those concerning performance standards, as are those which involve workloads. Unsurprisingly, the privatisation of probation has been a complex process, as one might expect when transferring assets from a public service like the Probation Service, with its range of duties and varying interests.

Privatisation operates in other parts of the public sector, including some in the criminal justice system, although not of course in the same form. During the 1980s parts of the Department of Work and Pensions were privatised. The aim there was to monitor unemployed persons and consequently reduce unemployment rates. This also provided the model of PbR which has been used in the privatisation of probation to pay the private sector providers. Whether such a scheme could be used elsewhere the criminal justice system is rather doubtful. Chris Grayling, who was Lord Chancellor and architect of much of the version of privatisation that eventually emerged on the statute book (and incidentally, involved in other privatisation programmes), does not thinks so, although he suggests it may be appropriate for juvenile justice. In this sense PbR is largely agency specific.

Although not unique to probation the form taken has of course been determined by the demands of criminal justice generally and probation in particular. Privatisation within the probation system has been markedly different from elsewhere including that of the Prison Service. So too have been the aims, which in the case of the prison system are in one sense less complex and more direct. Privatisation in the Prison Service began much earlier, where the aims were to overcome the spiralling costs of the prison system, and to ease the shortage of places – the prison population was reaching exceptional levels. Prison privatisation was concerned with introducing innovative management systems and reducing labour costs, with an overarching aim to break the monopoly power of the Prison Officers Association (POA). In probation it was different.[15] The problems involved in the privatisation of probation were to make a public service more effective and efficient, yet preserve some of its characteristics which have traditionally been at the centrepiece of the service. Unlike the Prison Service, the work of the Probation Service is not centred around one building, and its activities not so closely allied to one particular geographical centre.

A centre piece of privatisation in probation is PbR, one of the methods available for introducing privatisation into all government services. For at least a decade before the Probation Service was privatised the government made it clear it was committed to introducing PbR. Chris Grayling, the Secretary of State responsible for implementing PbR, has attracted most of the criticism, some seeing him as forcing through a policy as if it was his own personal view, and against the prevailing trend, but PbR was a central feature of government policy from the earlier years. Consider this from the Conservative Party in 2009:

> The principle of incentivising performance through Payment by Results, with success based on the absence of reoffending, should be introduced for prisons, the providers of community sentences, and the providers of rehabilitation programmes, - whether in the public private or voluntary sector. With devolved responsibilities and new incentives, we can create a revolution in how offenders are managed, and drive down reoffending.[16]

This manifesto promise was carried through to the Coalition Government and privatisation of probation occurred in 2014. The main platform to PbR is that rehabilitation services will be paid according to how successful they are in reducing reoffending. A basic tariff is paid to cover their costs and an additional tariff paid if targets to reduce reoffending are met.[17] As such it fits the demands of government to reduce costs. As will be shown later, reducing probation practices to economic modelling may sound disarmingly simple, but they turn out to be alarmingly complex. There are problems of a definitional nature, i.e. how to define success, problems about obtaining data and problems of attribution, i.e. who is responsible for any success that might be achieved. Identifying causal connections in criminal justice is no less difficult than in all other forms of behaviour, except in this case it means that establishing links that leads to the payment (or not) for results is even more complex, as they often depend on information from other sources, i.e. the police and the courts.

Objections to privatisation

Privatisation, along with neo liberalism generally, is not without its critics. Objections have come in various forms and with differing degrees of intensity. Most critics come from the public sector itself, where there is often an in-built hostility to the private sector generally, and to the profit motive in particular, which is seen as unacceptable to a public service. Related objections are that criminal justice is not a commodity that can be reduced to its component parts which can be sold to make profits for shareholders. It is a public service, and as such provides the means by which the state protects its citizens. In contrast, supporters of neo liberalism see these objections as merely ways of extending and promoting inefficient systems which support a self seeking group of public sector employees. The debate is likely to continue, and remains at the centre of the privatisation of probation

Some opponents have taken a holistic view and simply object to all forms of privatisation, and outsourcing too, whether they be in Levels 2 or 3. They have done so on a matter of principle and simply state there is no place for the private sector within the public sector generally, or in the Probation Service in particular. Others have been more circumspect, objecting to certain aspects but not others. That is to say, they may see a place for some aspects of Level 1 privatisation (such as introducing better management systems), but go no further and would object to the transfer of assets away from the public sector. Others, may have few objections to privatisation in Levels 2 and 3, or may object to one and not the other. The permutations are endless, the point being there is no hard and fast view, and little or no agreement about what is or is not acceptable.

Those taking the more extreme view invariably start with the assertion that private sector involvement, which means promoting profits, is unsatisfactory, perhaps immoral, and against the basic principles of public service. For example, the playwright Alan Bennett, in a Foreword to *The golden age of probation*, says "Probation belongs at a local level and profit should not come into it. The satisfactions of the Probation Service are not financial ones and nor should they be; they are the rewards of dedication and service."[18] "Profit" in this context is contrasted with those "satisfactions of the service" which comes from its vocational calling. And in a petition presented in 2014 entitled "Do not privatise the Probation Service," petitioners believed that those convicted by a criminal court should only be supervised by those employed by a publicly accountable Probation Service. This objection to privatisation relies on an assertion that "profit" is placed at one end of the continuum and "public service" at the other. And where this is so, then the debate is over. "Profit," as in the example above, becomes a pejorative term and no amount of discussion resolves that. In which case there is a straightforward dichotomy which views all public sector activities as good, and all private sectors as bad.

A slightly different approach, but producing a no less trenchant opposition, has been to object to the use of the private sector in all forms of public service which involve criminal justice, but not other parts of the public sector; criminal justice having certain features which render it different from other forms of public service, namely that it involves the state and the punishment of offenders. So, to introduce privatisation into criminal justice is said to take away the state's responsibility for dealing with those who break its laws. This view asserts that criminal justice is qualitatively different from all other government services. The argument goes something like this; the state asserts its power and authority through the criminal justice system and it is the task of those who administer that service, which uniquely involves administering punishment, to distance itself from the private sector whose main aim is to produce profit for its shareholders. Rather, they, and this includes the Probation Service, should be part of the apparatus of the state concerned only with such matters as demanded by the state, and not be distracted by other demands. This argument is based on a quasi-jurisprudential position that only the state should deal with those who break its laws. If that assertion is retained then of course the central premise remains; that the transfer of functions away from the public sector is undesirable in principle. That is to say, responsibility should not be shelved or passed to others, especially to private contractors. It is a view which extols the strength and importance of public service within the public sector. It distinguishes between a *public* service and *a* service, a difference which also dominates the debate.

This is a view of a public service which has retained considerable support. So much so that some of the most enthusiastic supporters of privatisation might see that some areas of criminal justice should not be privatised; the courts being an obvious example. The courts, according to this argument, have and should remain aloof because we ask of them that they present and preserve a dignity of office, and in doing so guarantee impartiality, independence, and confidentiality. This being so we cannot have offenders being sentenced by those who are not independent, or who may pass sentences in ways that support their own self-interest – as has happened in the USA in some of their "problem solving courts" where a judge sentenced an offender to a programme in which he had a financial interest. Nor can we have those passing sentence who are not impartial; or not seen to be impartial, or not able to respect the confidentiality of those who appear before them. Or as far as the Probation Service is concerned, preparing a court report by someone who is biased towards a specific organisation, and the report writer likely to obtain advantage by slanting the report towards the report writers self-interest. It is a position that retains considerable support, suggesting there are limits to the introduction of privatisation in criminal justice, and of course to some critics that limit has already been reached.

The National Association of Probation Officers (NAPO) takes a slightly different view, in that it sees privatisation of probation as creating a false or pseudo market. It says the government's aim with privatisation was for potential suppliers of offender services to compete with each other to bring down costs. But for NAPO the normal economic laws of supply and demand do not operate in a situation which involve the supervision of offenders. Who for example is the customer? Is it the offender? This, according to NAPO, is doubtful. The offender cannot chose his/her supervisor and this being so, the normal customer relationship does not apply. The court is not the customer either, nor is the Probation Service or the government. Hence NAPO's view is that privatisation creates a false market.[19]

NAPO follows this up with a more general criticism of privatisation by providing a list of previous failures, concluding that there is little evidence that privatisation has added any value to the provision of offender services. It offers a number of examples which occurred in the bidding process for the privatisation of probation, highlighting one where two major companies were excluded because of their poor records dealing with offender populations. (These were SERCO and G4S who following a Ministry of Justice investigation into Electronic Monitoring Contracts, were excluded from the bidding process.) NAPO gives other examples such as where the privatisation of bail services was given to a private company with no previous experience of offender populations. This contract went dramatically wrong, such that within weeks the Ministry of Justice was inundated with complaints of lack of supervision, rowdy behaviour, and drug taking. The contract was cancelled and given to the voluntary sector.

Following this level of attack Ken Collett, an ex Chief Probation Officer from Cheshire, wrote in a letter to *The Guardian* (no date): "I can only conclude that decency, compassion and humanity towards those who commit crimes, and the belief that sustained assistance can turn their lives around now too old fashioned and stand in the way of profits and global business." Others saw the Probation Service as "an island of decency," and self evidently worth preserving. For example, Lord Ramsbotham[20] in the House of Lords Debate showed his support for a Probation Service in its traditional form when he said "At the heart of the distinct role of the Probation Service within the criminal justice system is person-to-person supervision and the rehabilitation of offenders in the community."

The general march of events meant Lord Ramsbotham, and others similarly inclined, were out of step. They was asking to retain the *status quo* and given the government's eagerness for change there was little chance of that. There might have been a possibility to halt or redirect the move towards privatisation, and there may have been a possibility of changing course, but not to return to what there was before. Such supporters in the debate were fewer in number, most others saw the service as an expensive irrelevance, as unable to meet the demands of an ever changing world, and out of step with events. Too often, they would say, Probation Officers' interpretations of the offender's behaviour were unrealistic, sometimes bordering on sentimentality, and offering less an interpretation of offending behaviour and more of an excuse. A new view was beginning to emerge, which saw the offender as more responsible for his/her actions, making choices to offend. When "Tough on crime, tough on the causes of crime" became New Labour's watchword it meant providing less help and support, but more supervision and control.

Introduction 19

Many supporters of privatisation believed that reforms of the Probation Service were long overdue. It was seen as requiring some form of modernisation which would involve introducing new and more efficient practices. Mike Hough, for example talks of "public sector bureaucracies which grow into powerful self serving bodies with an inflexible management and workforce." In this he was clearly alluding to the Probation Service, which he says has failed to drive up performance.[21] These criticisms were invariably part of a wider critique, especially from government, who have argued that privatisation was essentially beneficial, whether it be to the organisation itself, or to the wider public, and that included the taxpayers. Critics of the service saw it as failing to meet modern standards of an "effective, efficient, and economically improved public service."

These criticisms were mostly formulated as an attack on a traditional way of working. In the early 1980s they were directed at its poor administration and poor record keeping, but above all on its failure to reduce reconvictions. Its critics included a number of more recent Home Secretaries, for example John Reid, who later, in 2007, said the Probation Service was "not fit for purpose," and "not working as well as it should."[22] Or Ken Clarke, in 2011, who suggested that the riots of that year were the consequence of a failure in offender rehabilitation.

Critics could point to some success with earlier attempts at privatisation. Alison Leibling, discussing the privatisation of prisons, says there is evidence that high performing private sector prisons generally do well at providing activity, meeting targets, and treating prisoners with respect. She says prisoners report better staff–prisoner relationships in many private prisons with prisoner well-being higher than in those in the public sector.[23] Of course such comparisons are inappropriate in their way, one important difference is that privatisation in prisons raised staff morale; in probation it lowered it.

In spite of numerous objections the government has continued with the privatisation programme. It has pushed it through, justifying it as a means of change, and in doing so remodelling the Probation Service and changing it into a mixture of public and private services. The overall aim has always been to make it more effective, more efficient and better managed. The question is has it succeeded, or has it all been a mistake which will take decades to put right?

In what follows I want to describe these and numerous other changes, and ask how they came about and what effect have they had on the service. I want to look closely at what privatisation means, and how this particular version has been introduced, how it works, and of course to what effect. There are also more general questions to be asked, notably what does privatisation mean to the criminal justice system generally, and are there lessons to be learned from this? Also, I want to see privatisation as a process which began at some earlier period and is expected to continue; the Ministry of Justice has suggested that there will be modifications to procedures as so called "teething troubles" have occurred. At the time of writing (July 2018) changes have already taken place, some as a result of criticisms others through events; one of which is The Prisons and Courts Act which will, for the first time, require prisons to emphasise rehabilitation, requiring prisons to reform and rehabilitate offenders as well as punish them. This will immediately affect the Probation Service now and in the future. But the most important change comes in a Ministry of Justice publication, *Strengthening probation, building confidence* (2018), which announced that the contracts for the CRCs will be ended earlier – in 2020 and not 2022, and the Government will invest a further £22m per annum to improve the quality of services.[24] This is clearly an on going saga likely to continue for some time.

Format of the book

The format of the book is as follows. First, the areas to be covered: we begin in Chapter 2 with the government's intervention; then, in Chapter 3, assess the Probation Services' reaction to this; and in Chapters 4 and 5 examine privatisation itself and see what it means to the Probation Service. A sixth, final section is about the possibility of the Probation Service remaining or perhaps developing into a new type of court based service.

Specifically, in Chapter 2 this means looking at a history of government proposals leading up to the most important proposal in January 2013, *Transforming Rehabilitation: a revolution in the way we manage offenders*. This set out the government's plans for privatisation. Government intervention, although persistent throughout the last 50 years, was initially light, concerned mainly with training and funding. Later, the aim was more direct, aimed at promoting change and reducing cost, mostly fed by the government's reaction to higher crime rates. There were also the problems with new forms of crime such as drug abuse, terrorism, cybercrime etc.

Numerous White Papers made the same point; that existing services need to do more, cost less, and become more effective. In the 1980s however government pressure increased; it began to seek even more cost effective services, which as far as probation was concerned inevitably meant additional control over its expenditure. Also the government wanted evidence to show that probation works, i.e. reduces crime.

Chapter 3 shows the Probation Service's reaction to these demands. The general conclusion is that it seemed either unable or unwilling to respond. It clung to its vision of a service providing a therapeutic response to the offender's personal circumstances. As such it began to be outdated and left behind by events. Or if not by events, then certainly by the new type of offenders. Drug users, for example, were rarely suitable candidates for therapy, nor, whilst they were using drugs, did they want it. Worse than that, the service failed to show it was able to be cost effective and/or reduce criminality. And so, convinced of its own rectitude it failed to meet the demands imposed upon it, and failed to live up to others expectations. It became ripe for change, especially by a government eager to control expenditure. It failed to produce the necessary solutions asked of it, and failed to accept what was being demanded of it.

In Chapters 4 and 5 I want to look more closely at what privatisation means and ask what this has done to the Probation Service. There is no doubt the change has been enormous. It has created immense problems for all, whether working as Probation Officers in the traditional sense, or for those working for the CRCs. I want to look at the way CRCs are funded. ("Payment by Results" is the catchphrase, but what is a "result" and how and when are payments made?) The privatisation of the Probation Service is a complex matter but there is much evidence to suggest the service, or rather what is left of it, has come off badly, and the CRCs have done poorly as well. Whether the offenders have benefitted is another matter.

In the final chapter I ask if the Probation Service can ever recover from such changes. Or rather; is probation still possible? And is privatisation reversible, or if not, then can it be modified in ways which return to some aspects of the probation ideal? I want to offer some suggestions as to what a future Probation Service might look like, what sort of role it might play in the criminal justice system, and about its future generally. Most of all, I want to ask whether any future government is sufficiently interested to seek a future for it.

Notes

1 This by Professor Sir Leon Radzinowicz, later Professor at the University of Cambridge, Institute of Criminology.
2 Of course to talk of a "Golden Age" is misleading if only because it may not have existed, or if it did then there will be differences of opinion as to when it occurred. "Golden Ages" usually occurred at some point either just before one was born or during some early stages of one's career. My interpretation of this 'Golden Age' was during my own period as Probation Officer in Inner London in the 1960s.
3 House of Commons (2014) *Crime reduction policies: a coordinated approach? Interim report on the Government's Transforming Rehabilitation programme.* HC 1004.
4 Andrew Selous. Letter to Steve Brine MP, 16th March 2015.
5 Ministry of Justice (2013) *Transforming Rehabilitation: a revolution in the way we manage offenders. A strategy for Reform.* Cm 8619. This was preceded by a Green Paper *Breaking the cycle: effective punishment, rehabilitation and sentencing of offenders* in 2010.
6 The Government White Paper HMSO (2014) *Transforming Rehabilitation: a strategy for reform* was later transformed into the 2014 Offender Rehabilitation Act.184.
7 Ministry of Justice (2010) *Breaking the cycle: effective punishment, rehabilitation and sentencing of offenders.* (Cm 7972). Para. 23. This was a Green Paper published in December which included plans for Payment by Results and a commitment to introduce these features to all providers by 2015. In January 2013 the government published a *Summary of Responses* to the above.
8 See Mair G and Burke L (2012) *Redemption, rehabilitation and risk management: a history of probation.* Routledge. Pg. 178 and 184.
9 Reported in NAPO (2011) *Briefing paper: resistance to cuts and privatisation.*
10 Cannings J (2014) A view of probation in the 1960s: from the bottom. In Statham R (ed) *The golden age of probation.* Waterside Press, pp, 97–106. Pg. 98.
11 Ministry of Justice (2010) op. cit. P. 10.
12 Stacey C (2012) The marketization of the Criminal Justice System: who is the customer? *Probation Journal.* Vol. 59, No. 4, pp. 406–414.
13 Courier Mail 1st January 2018. Pg. 12.
14 Faulkner D pers. com.
15 Ludlow A. (2014) Transforming Rehabilitation. What lessons can be learned from prison privatisation? *European Journal of Probation.* Vol. 6, No.1, pp. 67–81.
16 Conservative Party (2009) *Prisons with a purpose: our sentencing and rehabilitation revolution to break the cycle of crime.* Pg. 16.
17 Fox C and Albertson K (2012) Is Payment by Results the most efficient way to address the challenges faced by the criminal justice sector? *Probation Journal.* Vol. 59, No. 4, pp. 355–373. Pg. 359.
18 Bennett A (2014) Foreword. In Statham R (ed) *The golden age of probation* op. cit.

19 NAPO (2012) Briefing paper. Probation privatisation and accountability.
20 House of Lords Debates. Hansard 21st December 2010. Cm 1143.
21 Hough M (2006) Introduction. In Hough M, Allen R, and Padel U (eds) *Reshaping probation and prisons*. Policy Press, pp. 1–7.
22 The latter quote from BBC News 2006. See Mair G and Burke L (2012) op. cit. Pg. 175.
23 Leibling A (2006) Lessons from prison privatisation for probation. In Hough M, Allen R, and Padel U (eds) *Reshaping probation and prisons*. Policy Press. pp. 69–77.
24 See Ministry of Justice (2018) *Strengthening probation, building confidence*, Cm 9613, and the corresponding impact assessment related to the above.

2

GOVERNMENT INTERVENTION

We are talking of England and Wales. The position in Scotland and Northern Ireland is different. In Scotland in 1964 the Probation Service was largely disbanded after the Kilbrandon Report, and the juvenile court replaced with a system of children's hearings. It was then merged with the social work departments, perhaps a foretaste or omen of what was to come in England and Wales.

Where to begin? I have chosen the starting point as the late 1960s, when paradoxically the Probation Service seemed to be at its height. Then no one talked of privatisation. The Probation Service was a government agency, publicly funded, experiencing its "Golden Age." Yet it is possible to see signs of what was to come, and with the passing decades detect a trend. This is of course with the benefit of hindsight, in those early days there was never a thought, let alone a fear about the future.

What is remarkable however, is how everything has moved in one direction; almost as if toward a predetermined conclusion. The pieces seem to fit. Each piece, or change in policy, seemed to be preparing the way for the next stage, with each piece fitting into that predetermined jigsaw. From the "Golden Age" to privatisation there seemed something inexorable about what happened. Accordingly, I have selected those features which suggest a move in that direction, a move towards a new and influential paradigm, that of neo liberalism, or if not a direct move then actions by government which paved the way for a neo liberal conclusion. The journey towards privatisation appears to have been deliberate, where, if not always articulated as such, nonetheless can be seen in terms of a single linear movement.

The period under discussion is divided into three separate sections. The first begins at the "Golden Age" in the late 1960s and goes up to the 1991 Criminal Justice Act. This is the period in which the first set of controls or restrictions were placed on the Probation Service. It was also the time when the government began introducing its ideas about efficiency and effectiveness into public services. The second period lasted for just over a decade and goes up to the Carter Review in 2003. This review, accepted by government, changed the face of the Probation Service with its recommendations for contestability, which in effect meant introducing the service to contracts from private firms and the voluntary sectors. The third period was from the Carter Review to privatisation in 2014 and beyond. I say "beyond" because the debate continues, aided by reports from the Probation Inspectorate and others on the workings of the privatised service.

Stage one: The "Golden Age" to the 1991 Act

In the first stage, i.e. in the so called "Golden Age," the Probation Service was involved in a wide range of services, including being a central figure in the juvenile court. That meant providing reports, supervising children on probation, as well as being involved in family proceedings such as *Guardian ad litem* in adoption and disputes over custody. It was the loss of these services which heralded the important changes that were to come, and it is doubtful if the service ever recovered. The loss of the juvenile court came in the late 1960s when large sections of the juvenile justice system were handed to the newly formed local authority social work department (after the White Paper *Children in Trouble* and the Seebohm Report on the organisation of social services). The legal position was reaffirmed by the 1969 Children and Young Persons Act, which introduced supervision orders for children under the age of 17. The impact and corresponding loss was irreparable. In the late 1960s just under half of all Probation Orders made were on juveniles (about 47%) and nearly all reports on juveniles were done by the Probation Service.

There was a loss too of personnel. The new local authority social work department created after the Seebohm Report attracted some Probation Officers. Some moved because they were interested in the care and supervision of children, others because they believed the loss of the juvenile justice system had pushed the Probation Service away from its social work heritage and more towards criminal justice. In this of course they were correct. It was a significant loss, producing a significant change of direction. Still others were attracted by the prospects of promotion where it was more difficult in the Probation Service. Probation Officers who remained in the service were however quick to point out that promotion in the social services departments was offset by conditions of service; the Probation Service was less bureaucratic and offered more independence. Also, Probation Officers had a direct responsibility for their caseloads in ways seemingly impossible for those working for the local authority.

There were however numerous gains, albeit not necessarily in a direction that was thought beneficial to some members of the service. Nonetheless it was beginning to be appreciated that with the service losing many of its court based social work duties, it was moving in a direction away from its traditional view of rehabilitation. The loss of juvenile justice therefore was not simply a loss of function, but it represented a loss of traditional probation and social work values.

The attack on probation social work values began in the late 1960s. The criminal justice system generally, and the Probation Service in particular, was dominated by a version of rehabilitation which was primarily about offenders receiving treatment for their criminality. The problem of crime was seen as a problem of defective personal relationships. For probation, the training, and desired forms of practice, was "social casework" – in essence a form of psychotherapy. Casework was about providing insights into the offender's character, which would be expected to produce a positive effect on future behaviour.

This form of rehabilitation was being attacked from different sides. First, there were those who saw it as "theoretically faulty, systematically discriminating and inconsistent with justice." These critics challenged the level of involvement casework required in the offenders' personal lives. This was justified by the caseworker as necessary for successful therapy, yet critics saw it as deeply intrusive. They also saw it as providing excessive power and control to the caseworker. This in turn became translated as a threat to civil rights, which came from the powers and control granted to the so-called gatekeepers, i.e. those who made decisions about treatment, about the length of time to be detained for treatment, and the often arbitrary nature of their decisions. "Sentenced to be helped" was one of the anti rehabilitation slogans of the time, which implied that those being sentenced/helped were unwelcome receivers of the rehabilitative response. "Choose your Probation Officer with care" was another, for the treatment provided, the (in)frequency of contact, and the decision to initiate breach proceedings for those failing to meet requirements, were all seen as more to do with the actions of the Probation Officer than the offender. Films such as *One flew over the cuckoo's nest* also depicted the malevolent side of rehabilitation and the dangers to those who were not prepared to accept the rehabilitative model. It depicted too the powers of those who operated it. The solution? Radical non-intervention or simply, a demand to leave people alone.[1] Or, if this was not acceptable, and some form of intervention required, then a return to the justice model with retribution as the demanding principle such as "just deserts," or to a Benthamite model of deterrence. Rehabilitation was seen as against principles of justice; it opened the way for decisions, not about the offence, but about the offender's personality.

Yet Probation Officers, trained and ardent supporters of that treatment model, did not see themselves in this way. They saw probation as being on the side of the offender. They did so within a framework written into legislation which was to "advise, assist and befriend." Debates about Probation Officers being malevolent or control agents, or both, seemed irrelevant at best, and erroneous at worst.

The second attack came from a different direction and was about the effectiveness of probation. Did it reduce offending, and where was the evidence to support the Probation Services' claims that it did? This was the so-called "Nothing Works?" debate, not to be confused with the later "What Works?" which asked similar questions but in a slightly less challenging form. The "Nothing Works?" debate was less of a debate, more of an assertion that probation had no discernible impact on reconviction rates. Specifically, this attack on probation came from a small amount of research, most of it from the Home Office Research Unit, that showed probation was no more effective, in terms of reconviction rates, than fines or discharges. This was so, even with low risk offenders. Other research, such as that reported by Roger Hood and Richard Sparks, confirmed this. They said in their seminal work *Key issues in criminology* [2] that fines and discharges are, in fact, more effective than was probation for reducing reconviction rates or indeed, imprisonment for first offenders. Hardly a recommendation for probation.

The response from probation was interesting. Generally speaking, it simply ignored these results. Or if it considered them at all, its officers rebutted them as being due to difficulties under which they worked, e.g. excessively large caseloads. Smaller caseloads, they said, would allow more time to be spent with their "clients" and thereby improve matters.[3] When later research showed that smaller caseloads failed to produce better results, they countered this by saying it was because of too much time being spent on needless administration. But the damage was done. When later research in the 1990s showed that probation and rehabilitation was occasionally effective, it was too late. The service never fully recovered from the first set of reported failings. It had lost some of its lustre and never regained it.[4]

Yet at the time, research, especially government research, was intended more to provide assistance rather than denigrate. When the service had been so imperious it came as something of a surprise to be told that fines or discharges were equally effective, if not more so than probation. These results could not be ignored, and in fact research results became a constant threat to the services' authority. The same problems arose some 50 years later when the Probation Service had to defend itself against similar criticisms of effectiveness, except in this latter period failure to convince led to reductions in government funding. In these earlier times, when the service could not show it was effective in reducing criminality, it only lost some of its credibility. Yet it needed to change, and to do so rapidly.

The introduction of the Community Service Order was another key feature of the early 1970s and was another of those threats. The Community Service Order simply challenged the Probation Order as the dominant force as an alternative to custody. When introduced by Barbara Wootton, the architect of the scheme, it was described as "difficult to determine, as it was neither wholly punitive nor wholly rehabilitative." In fact, she said the chameleon type quality was also its strength. She believed the Probation Service would have a major role to play in determining its future, if only because the Probation Service would determine the extent of its use by the courts.[5]

The first Community Service Order was made at Nottingham Crown Court on the 2nd January 1973. Community Service became one of those criminal justice penalties which the Probation Service never fully understood. Or if it did, and saw its significance, it rarely embraced it. Some Probation Officers were suspicious of the impact of the order on the future direction of community penalties. For although Community Service was a community penalty, and therefore well within the compass of the Probation Service (as opposed to that of say, the Prison Service) many within the Probation Service objected to what they saw as its punitive side. It also required a level of administration which was outside the traditional Probation Officer's role. Also, it meant working with an outside organisation, not something in which the Probation Service had shown much interest hitherto. What the Community Service Order did of course was undermine the monopoly position of the Probation Order which had been a standard feature of probation practice in the community for the last 50 years.

The Community Service Order (renamed the Community Punishment Order in 2001) was the first of a number of community orders aimed at providing a credible alternative to a custodial sentence.[6] Hitherto the Probation Order had been the mainstay of community sentences, but was not thought sufficiently inclusive to take account of those offenders not seeking a social work service, nor to offer repayment to the community for the damage done. In short it did not carry a sufficient threat of punishment to provide a credible alternative. Incidentally, the introductory legislation required a Community Service Order to be a sentence in its own right, and not a condition of a Probation Order. Were Community Service to be a condition of a Probation Order some Probation Officers would "mistakenly find themselves involved in forms of supervision difficult to reconcile with their professional consciences," i.e. too punitive for their liking.[7]

The demand for that "credible alternative" became a theme which dominated government thinking for the next decade. It was picked up in the 1991 Criminal Justice Act, and later developed and amended up to the time of privatisation in 2014. The service was always suspicious of Community Service for the reasons given above, but also because it thought these orders introduced the private sector into an otherwise public service. And by becoming part of that "seamless link," i.e. linking the community with custody, the Probation Service could be marginalised as the dominant force in community sentencing.

By the early 1980s an assessment of the overall picture would suggest the Probation Service was dented rather than damaged. It had survived the last two decades relatively unscathed, although still subject to quite severe challenges and criticism. However, the more serious damage was ahead, with a major challenge to the Probation Officer's authority. This came in 1984 with the Home Office "Statement of National Objectives and Priorities" (SNOP). The title was on the face of it innocuous, and at the time went almost unnoticed, yet it had serious implications. No one had spoken of a "National" Probation Service before.[8] Probation had always been administered through a separate set of local probation organisations, what one commentator calls "local fiefdoms." These were run by Chief Probation Officers who had hitherto controlled their local services (except for London which was administered differently). The introduction of a "national" service demoted those local chiefs to that of local managers. Not only was a "national service" an attack on these fiefdoms, but it made the service easier for governments to control.

The government followed this with a set of defined objectives, again a departure from the usual way of allowing the service to define its own aims and priorities. In the House of Lords debates Lord Harris of Greenwich said this was to be welcomed and then added "the probation service is primarily a criminal justice service" – not what the service necessarily wanted to hear.[9] The government drew attention to the cost of the service (6,000 Probation Officers, 5,000 ancillary staff costing £150m in 1983/84 and costing 5 times more than in 1963) and stressed the need to "interact with other agencies and other interests" including the Prison Service – all omens of what was to come. The National Association of Senior Probation Officers (NASPO) quoted by Lord Harris in the House of Lords Debate, got it right when they said,

> We see this statement as confirming the trend away from the ideals of the police court missionaries as epitomised by the phrase 'advise, assist and befriend' towards a more central role in the criminal justice system with its emphasis on the management of crime in the community.

As indeed it was, and confirmed by NAPO, later in 2011, who said that SNOP was the first attempt to bring the culture of business into the Probation Service.[10]

Another important proposal from SNOP was that it demanded consistency in record keeping, together with the better allocation of cases, better planning, more assessments involving risk management, and greater attention to the enforcement of the court's sentence. Details of these proposals were to appear later in National Standards for Offender Management, which set out the minimal amount of contact according to particular levels of risk. As such they were anathema to those who saw Probation Officers as autonomous professionals. Hitherto reporting etc. had been a matter to be decided by the Probation Officer, now there were a new set of rules and regulations, suggesting a form of managerialism, a style altogether new to the Probation Service. This was an unwelcome departure from existing practice, but again another foretaste of what was to come.

Whether so intended or not SNOP began to undermine the very basis of "advise, assist and befriend" which was the Probation Services' mantra, and one the service lived by, proudly proclaiming it as a justification for much of its practice. It meant what it said; give advice to offenders, help them over difficult times, and befriend them. "Advise, assist and befriend" allowed the Probation Service to claim it was on the side of the offender – even if as an official figure working for the courts it sometimes appeared otherwise. More than that it justified and articulated a way of working which promoted autonomy and discretion for the officer. It represented all that was described by critics as the *laissez faire* approach, where individual Probation Officers decided how often to see their clients, and what decisions were to be made about their future. It offered freedom for the clinician to decide on the forms of treatment to be offered, with an expectation that the government (or some other employing authority) would pick up the bill.

To many Probation Officers, "advise, assist and befriend" was the reason and justification for being an officer. It was what led them to enter the service. When that was attacked, and with it the autonomous probation culture that went with it, it was to the dismay of many. For example, some 50 years later, Joanna Hughes (Deputy Chair of NAPO in Gloucestershire) reporting on BBC File on Four, said of privatisation, "All the reasons I became a Probation Officer are destroyed."[11] Presumably she meant by that she could no longer make her own decisions about how to conduct her cases, and no longer be required to "advise, assist and befriend" them. SNOP was the first official document that began a lengthy process to undermine that culture and replace it with a stronger managerial style.

Finally, in this period there was the 1991 Criminal Justice Act. This was a comprehensive piece of legislation preceded by a government White Paper, *Punishment Custody and the Community* (1988).[12] The Act made a number of changes and introduced new measures, mainly relating to community punishments, where the aim was to provide that credible alternative to custody. One of the changes was to the status of the Probation Order, these were no longer to be "instead of sentencing," but a sentence in its own right. Again, on the face of it this did not appear important, only a minor change perhaps, yet it was a radical departure from earlier times. It placed the Probation Order at the same level as a Community Service Order or a Combination Order, the latter being an order which combines Probation Orders and Community Service Orders. Hitherto Probation Orders were set apart, perhaps seen as qualitatively different and rising above other community orders. Suddenly they became part of community punishments.

There were other changes to the Probation Order in the 1991 Act, no less radical and also indicating a further break from the past. The Act stipulates that a Probation Order should only be made, under Section 8(2)

> when the Court is of the opinion that the supervision of the offender by a probation officer is desirable in the interests of (a) securing the rehabilitation of the offender, and (b) protecting the public from harm or preventing the commission by him of further offences.

No "advise, assist or befriend" here but a demand that the order reduce crime and the Probation Service act as a crime reduction agency. All of which further put the Probation Service on a path in opposition to its earlier social work aspirations and roots.

There were four other sections of the 1991 Act, all of which appeared innocuous but again all turned out to be anything but that. There are:

Section 8.4 which gives powers to "the Secretary of State (that he) may enter into a contract with another person for the running of any prison;"

Section 11 (1) which gives powers to the court to make a Combination Order, that is to say "(a) be under the supervision of a probation officer for a period specified in the order, being not less than 12 months and not more than 3 years; and (b) to perform unpaid work for a number of hours so specified, being in the aggregate not less than 40 hours but not more than 100."

Section 13 (1) which gives powers to the court to make a curfew order which may "include requirements for securing the electronic monitoring of the offender's whereabouts during the curfew periods specified in the order."

Section 13 (3) to use electronic monitoring which "may include entering into contracts with other persons for the electronic monitoring by them of offenders' whereabouts."

In the first, the possibility that the government may privatise the prison system was a real threat and warning for the future. Within two years the first private prison was in operation.[13] Second, the introduction of "unpaid work" as part of a sentence involving a Probation Officer was another clear indication that the service was moving in that "punitive direction." The third and fourth points above refer to the introduction of electronic monitoring (or EM). Again, EM was another of those apparently insignificant changes introduced into legislation, almost unnoticed, yet which turned out to be massively significant, in this case because it introduced a Level 2 form of privatisation into a criminal justice service.

Of those legal changes listed above EM was the most important. It raised numerous questions, some of which are dealt with in a later chapter, but others are relevant here. EM was but another example of the way the Probation Service was hostile to change, and illustrates how it was unaware that new technology would play an increasingly important part of community justice programmes. EM illustrates the way the private sector became further entrenched into the British criminal justice system.[14] In doing so it produced another of those building blocks for privatisation

Although available in the late 1980s EM was very much a 1990s phenomenon. It was first introduced into the Probation Service in the late 1960s and early 1970s. Offenders on probation had traditionally been required to report to the Probation Officer, and EM is but another form or reporting, and by implication another form of control. Yet EM is more extensive; it can track the movement of offenders, help enforce curfews, assist with home detention, and help enforce bail. It was introduced in the USA in 1970 and spread to the UK where Mike Nellis reports it was enthusiastically supported by New Labour when Jack Straw proclaimed it to be the future of community punishment.[15]

There is little doubt that EM had a prominent role in the management of offenders. There were initial fears that it was part of a developing industry of corrections technology. The danger was that it would become part of a developing punitive culture supporting the ever increasing demands for populist punishments. Mike Nellis argues that in the long run it was traditional penalties like probation which were most weakened by such populist demands, but he also talks of an integrated offender rehabilitation programme where EM and traditional probation could have worked together. Rejecting EM says Nellis, gave an additional incentive to government to involve and empower the private sector, whose ambition to develop integrated justice services is well known. He adds, prophetically in 2003, that these integrated services "may yet have fateful consequences for probation itself."[16] It is a pity that the Probation Service did not listen, or see the merit of such a partnership.

The importance of EM as far as the privatisation of the service is concerned is that it again moved the service further away from its social work roots. It also introduced a potent form of outsourcing (Level 2) into the service. The opposition to EM came initially from NAPO, who this time found itself in agreement with the Association of Chief Officers of Probation (ACOP) the Police Federation and even most of the press.[17] The objection was basically that EM introduced a form of punishment into an area of corrections unused to such methods, but there were also objections about its supposed effectiveness as a likely measure to reduce the numbers of offenders in custody. The Home Office in turn saw it as dependable, and of course cheaper than prison. Nellis regards it as a means by which the Home Office was trying to press changes on the Probation Service, moving the emphasis from "social work with offenders" to "punishment in the community." The Probation Service, or rather many of its senior members, saw this too, and objected to the change. Nellis suggests however that many younger members were less hostile, seeing merit in the use of EM (also being more accepting of technology), but to NAPO all forms of EM were emblematic of all that the Probation Service should resist.[18]

EM was outsourced, with a small number of companies being responsible for most of the EM in England and Wales. This form of outsourcing was not just about introducing the private sector to the public sector, but a way of providing a potent form of managerialism which sought greater measures of control over offenders – and as it so happens over anyone else who was involved in running EM programmes. It created what Mike Nellis calls a climate more favourable to instruction and oversight than to discretionary human response.[19] This was due to an affinity between EM and managerialism, an affinity created by the very nature of EM itself.

This affinity has three aspects, all said to derive from the way in which EM can achieve managerialism's meticulous control over the offenders' movements. First it provides "control at a distance" in a way that Probation Officers cannot. Second it provides data (in a computerised form) which cannot be disputed. This data gives clear evidence of compliance and/or non compliance. Finally, it involves surveillance of the body, (as opposed to appeals to reason, conscience, or self-interest) which is a more complete form of surveillance than can be provided by human contact. Taken together these methods of control are superior to anything that can be provided by the Probation Officer, relying on personal accounts or reports from others on the activities of those under surveillance. The culture of managerialism, the monitoring by one means or another of specific requirements, is strengthened by this form of technical control, being much more acceptable to governments or anyone seeking to provide efficient and effective surveillance. It becomes another way of showing the traditional methods of the Probation Service were becoming redundant.

This was the end of the first stage where the building blocks of the traditional Probation Service were being dismantled and a new service was being established. Each new block was moving in the direction of and becoming more akin to the demands of neo liberalism. The loss of juvenile justice and of children's work in civil proceedings, and the thrust towards more offender based work was the first and most prominent examples. These were followed by other changes including the introduction of Community Service, and other community sentences, all placing them as sentences in their own right. The dye was cast. The next stage merely confirmed all that the traditionalists feared; that the Probation Service was to become neo liberal.

Stage two, and the Carter Report

The second stage goes up to the Carter Report, which was perhaps the most significant of all reports in terms of the privatisation of the service. This stage lasts from 1991 to 2003. The 1991 Act had been an important milestone in the way it changed the service from a social work service of the courts to a community based criminal justice service directed towards punishment in the community. This second stage is more about the politics of probation and the personalities involved. It is about those who pushed forward demands that the service become more efficient and effective – again moving it away from the direction most serving officers wished to go. Two Home Secretaries dominate, Michael Howard and Jack Straw, one Conservative, the other Labour, but hardly distinguishable in their ambitions to change the direction of the Probation Service.

I have selected a small number of features in this second stage, ignoring many others such as the debate on community sentences and the changes made to the training of its officers – the latter being discussed later. Taking an overview of the position, then the Probation Service entered the 1990s in a rather shaken condition. Whilst there was a general view in the courts that the service was doing well, and was trusted, probation practice had a certain vagueness about it, almost a mystical quality. The main problem; it was unable to show it was effective. This was to be one of its more significant and persistent failings. The other danger was that a Conservative Government, concerned about levels of public expenditure, was unlikely to be sympathetic to a service whereby it was required to write out the cheques (with some assistance from local authorities who also contributed to the funding) but with little control over how the money was spent. And the Probation Service was increasingly costly. George Mair and Lol Burke show that probation expenditure increased from £186.8m in 1985 to £286.7m in 1990/1, with the number of Probation Officers increasing from 6,220 to 7,153 over the same period. Caseloads however per officer decreased from 22.5 to 15.5 and the number of reports to the courts by main grade officers dropped from 69.1 to 50.9, also over that same period. The service expected new government initiatives, but the force with which these new demands were made and the changes imposed on the service was surprising.[20]

The 1990s were divided, politically into two areas; the first by a Conservative Government with Ken Clarke as Home Secretary from April 1992 to May 1993, followed by Michael Howard from May 1993 to May 1997. Then New Labour came to power with Jack Straw as Home Secretary. He was Home Secretary from May 1997 to June 2001 (see Appendix 1). I have selected three main areas for examination under the Conservative Government, the "Prison Works" speech of Michael Howard, the use of partnerships and the "What Works?" campaign. I have selected another two as important during Jack Straw's time in office, namely the creation of the National Probation Service in 2001, and the Carter Report in 2003.

The most daunting critique of the way the then contemporary system of criminal justice worked came at the Conservative Party Conference in 1993, when Michael Howard announced that "Prison Works," a view in direct opposition to traditional probation thinking. For if prison really does work, then why bother with probation? Or indeed with any other penal sanction, except of course for lowly offenders who would not commit further offences anyway? Michael Howard's answer to the increasing crime rates of the period were straightforward and simple; send as many offenders to prison as possible and the problem is thereby solved. Never mind the cost, this is the solution. So, in one swift move the Home Secretary believed crime rates could be reduced and the Probation Service bypassed. (That prison does not work, or rather works for only a very few, is neither here nor there.) In the Michael Howard scenario probation, with its competing vision of crime, simply stands outside the mainstream of criminal justice policy and practice. That it brought forth protests, especially from the Probation Service, was merely an irritant

If the Labour Government was expected to be more sympathetic to its cause then the Probation Service would be disappointed. Labour's manifesto in 1997 said New Labour must be modern, get value for money and get re-elected. Labour would be "tough on crime, tough on the causes of crime (it said this 3 times in the manifesto) as part of what it called a new approach to law and order. This was followed by statements such as "We insist on individual responsibility for crime" and "The Conservatives have forgotten the 'order' part of law and order." Admittedly the manifesto proclaimed that "we will attack the causes of crime by our measures to relieve social deprivation," but it also proudly announced that "Labour is the party of law and order in Britain today."[21] The aim was clear; there would be no return to the days when the offender was given a sympathetic hearing, and the Probation Service of old allowed to dominate the debate.

Michael Howard's period as Home Secretary from 27th May 1993, up to the arrival of the Labour Government on the 2nd May 1997, was characterised by a number of changes but nothing major in terms of legislation for the Probation Service. Two features showed the direction governments were moving: first that probation was being held more and more to account with a number of three year plans (from 1993 to 1997) providing more and more detailed performance indicators; second, that in 1995 in a Green Paper *Strengthening Punishment in the Community*[22] the government suggested a new single integrated community sentence replacing all others, and incorporating all the current orders (including the Probation Order) available in the adult courts.[23] These changes represent a move towards increasing levels of managerialism and punishment in the community. None of which appealed to the Probation Service.

There were occasional flashes whereby the Probation Service tried to meet current demands and respond to Michael Howard's critique and become a more acceptable organisation – acceptable that is to what was perceived as such by an unsympathetic government. A major initiative aimed at meeting its critics was to increase the use of partnerships. Partnerships were a key feature of the 1990s, and represent Levels 2 and 3 on the privatisation scale. Some probation areas such as Inner London had to spend 10 % of their budget with NGOs, extracting a significant toll on their resources, others about 5%. Partnerships, which involved working closely with other agencies, were never popular within the Probation Service. Judith Rumgay said their use was often "reluctant, uneven and based selectively on a mixture of political imperatives and territorial preferences".[24] Nonetheless, where partnerships were used they often involved ground breaking work, with programmes such as offending behaviour, domestic violence, anger management, and sex offending being the most often used. These were reviewed from time to time, and assessed by researchers, independent of the Home Office and the Probation Service, although the driving force was almost always the Home Office where the aim was to find better models of risk assessment.

Although partnerships were used successfully in Inner London where over 50 were used in the treatment of drug users, the Probation Service's response varied. Contracting out work in the form of partnerships were seen as threats to the jobs of probation staff. Another objection was that partnerships weakened the image of the officer as an independent professional. The government's view was that no single service could be expected to solve the problem of crime; collaboration was therefore the only way forward

The Probation Service also had to meet an increasingly shrill political argument that the role of the state was not to provide services that could be more effectively and cheaply delivered by the private or voluntary sector. Jane Dominey[25] points out that the Probation Service was not excluded from this critique; nor was it any longer the sole resource for work with offenders in the community. The private and voluntary sectors had demonstrated they had equal skills which could be called upon, to be used either in partnerships, or as sole workers. This was not a claim welcomed by the Probation Service. Most of all there was within it a hint of privatisation, which had appeared more often than was thought comfortable. The Labour Government, for example, had made it clear it would extend the prison privatisation programme. Was probation next?

Another small and apparently innocent change occurred when the so called "consent" requirement to the Probation Order was removed under the Crime (Sentences) Act 1997 (under Section 38 (2)(a)). Hitherto offenders placed on probation always had to agree – some did not, but this was a dangerous choice, the alternative was never spelt out and could be prison, or perhaps offenders could be lucky and the alternative was a fine. Nonetheless the loss of the consent feature, almost a shibboleth of probation practice, was a serious challenge to the status and position of the Probation Order. It made it indistinguishable from other community penalties. (Under Section 38 3 (4) b the consent feature still applied to those being treated under a Probation Order for a mental disorder or a drug problem where "the offender must express his willingness to comply with such requirements.") Such a change had the important effect of undermining and removing key features of what Probation Officers saw as central to their work. Outsiders may have seen this as unimportant, but not most practicing officers.

The so called "What Works?" initiative was another such attempt to stave off criticism – not to be confused with a similar sounding slogan "Nothing Works?" which appeared earlier in the 1970s, although one grew as a direct result of the other. "Nothing Works?" was a misrepresentation of an article by Robert Martinson in 1974, though one with considerable effect.[26] What Martinson actually said was that "with few and isolated exceptions the rehabilitative efforts that have been reported so far have had no appreciable effect on recidivism."[27] but it was interpreted and promoted as "Nothing Works?" This was quickly accepted and fitted into a then contemporary negative view of any attempt at rehabilitation. It became promoted to a "Nothing Works?" mantra covering all areas of criminal justice. Unsurprisingly, this percolated down to the Probation Service although George Mair and Lol Burke say it had little effect on individual practitioners: "… they seem to have been unaware of the message that what they were doing was ineffective, – and they carried on trying to rehabilitate offenders."[28] Mair and Burke make the point however that "Nothing Works?" had a significant impact on policy makers and researchers,[29] including those concerned with probation, creating a pessimism about its effectiveness which remained for decades.

With a general view among criminologists, policy makers, and others that "Nothing Works?" and an assertion by a Home Secretary that only "Prison Works," the Probation Service was not well placed to face the corresponding criticisms. "Nothing Works?" had a clear simplicity, which was well suited to the pessimism of the times, coming as it did in the early 1970s after sustained attacks on rehabilitation. In contrast the "What Works?" programme came as a relief when at last there was something to show that something did actually work, and above all, worked for the Probation Service. There is some dispute however as to its overall impact, some commentators are enthusiastic, others less so, but there is no dispute that it changed probation practice, albeit only for a short time before the service was overtaken by other, more pressing events. George Mair and Lol Burke say that the "What Works?" programme came to be sufficiently important to represent probation's only hope for survival.[30] That it lasted only for a few years from the mid 1990s until a decade or so later, shows the "turbulent times" in which the service found itself and a belief that it was reaching "the end of the road."[31]

Briefly, the "What Works?" programme was aimed at producing an evidence based initiative derived from cognitive behavioural therapy. Some probation areas were in the forefront of this development, Inner London being one, but others remained less convinced. The initial impetus came from Canada and involved a mixture of academics and practitioners using cognitive behavioural therapy in Canadian prisons. Their results were such as to show certain measures of success. These were presented to a number of probation services in England and Wales where the message was to argue against the "Nothing Works?" approach and show that their approach, cognitive behavioural therapy, did work with offenders. The "What Works?" programme was actively embraced by the Home Office, albeit that it was used primarily in prisons in Canada and therefore not directly transferrable to a system of probation in England and Wales. As George Mair points out, working with offenders in the community presents a different range of challenges that tended to be forgotten.[32] Nonetheless using meta analysis, a statistical technique involving analysis of a large collection of individual studies, the results claimed to show the "What Works?" programmes to have a measure of success.

There remains considerable debate about the overall impact of "What Works?" and it is interesting to speculate on its likely impact had Michael Howard remained Home Secretary. George Mair says its major effect was to provide the Probation Service with a national programme, and made Probation Officers feel positive about themselves, but overall the results were not encouraging. It may have given the Probation Service an increased credibility and a new public profile, and helped change the culture from a welfare orientated service, albeit for a short time, but it promised more than it achieved.[33]

The Labour Party's return to office in 1997 brought another programme of change, although as it happens not one markedly different from the Conservative's as far as criminal justice was concerned. The first and most important piece of legislation for the new government was the 2000 Criminal Justice and Court Services Act. I list below five features of this legislation, including the preceding White Paper, all of which had a direct effect on the Probation Service. The overall effect was the Act moved the service in the direction of greater central control (and consequently less autonomy) and even further away from its social work roots towards an increasing involvement in criminal justice.

1. The White Paper produced a threat, or if not a threat then certainly a fearful suggestion. It was about the ways prison and probation ought to work more closely together. A consultation paper, *Joining Forces to Protect the Public*, was issued in August 1998. It said a merger between prison and probation would improve the protection of the public and reduce re-offending. It did not say how or why. Nevertheless as a result of subsequent consultations with various parties the Home Secretary decided that the two services should not combine. However, the Explanatory Note to the legislation added somewhat darkly that "whilst the services should retain their separate identities they should use complementary methods to achieve these common goals." It was clear what it

implied. This was unwelcome to a service unused to working with other agencies, let alone the prison service with which it had little in common. It was left to the Carter Report some four years later to restate the argument.

2. The legislation covered renaming the "Probation Order," that staple of the service since its inception, to be called the "Community Rehabilitation Order" (under Section 43). (Two other orders were also renamed; the Community Service Order was to be called the Community Punishment Order, and the Combination Order to be called the Community Punishment and Rehabilitation Order (Under Sections 44 and 45).) If this was an attempt to be modern it failed. The practical effect was nominal – the change seems to be largely ignored. Courts still talk of the "Probation Order" as if nothing has changed. Yet the symbolic effect was huge. The government's intentions were clear, and the direction of its thinking was obvious.

3. The creation of the "National Probation Service for England and Wales" was also highly significant. The Explanatory Note to accompany the legislation puts the position thus: "in the case of the Probation Service, the Home Secretary decided that the aim should be to protect the public and to reduce re-offending through the effective enforcement of community sentences." It was, however, concluded that the existing arrangements under the Probation Service Act 1993, which provides for 54 separate probation services, were not conducive to the efficient and successful achievement of this aim.

Part 1 of the Act restructures the Probation Service and creates a unified service to be renamed the National Probation Service for England and Wales (NPS). On 1st April 2001 the NPS was created. The new service was to be directly accountable to the Home Secretary. Up to 2001 the 54 probation services had been independent bodies corporate. Local authorities were represented partly because of their financial contribution but also because of local interest. They were now reduced to 42 probation areas. The overall structure was based on those 42 local areas, each with a local probation board composed of representatives of the local community who understand local needs. Interestingly, enough the boundaries of these areas would match those of the police forces and the CPS, again making clear the direction in which the Government wished the service to go. The structure was also designed as a step towards the government's stated aim which was to improve efficiency by creating common boundaries across all the agencies in the criminal justice system. The NPS and the 42 boards were created in order to bring about what it called "greater consistency and rigour in policy and practice." The result was predictable. The 54 local probation chiefs suddenly became local probation office managers under a new "National Probation Service," with a national director. It was described as a "definite act of centralism," turning it into a service able to be controlled and administered by central Government under a "National" banner. Commentators such as George Mair and Lol Burke said it was a "profoundly important development,"[34] for the service lost its local autonomy, and of course its local control.

The local probation boards could employ staff or make other contractual arrangements for the delivery of the services for which they were responsible. The Act gave powers to the Home Secretary to appoint members of those local probation boards, and appoint the Chief Officer of each area. The Chief Officer would be able to give directions to boards, and through them to their own chief officers, as to how they fulfil their statutory responsibilities. In other words introduce a structure which permits more direct central government control.

Incidentally, the 'What Works?' programme was intimately bound up with the creation of the NPS. Indeed George Mair says it is both cause and effect.[35] That is to say a national programme requires a national service, and a national service requires a national programme. He says "Without the existence of a national probation service 'What Works?' could not have existed." Had "What Works?" been introduced to 54 separate probation services it is likely that its implementation would have been partial, inconsistent and resisted.[36]

4. The Probation Service was no longer required to provide welfare reports and supervise "endangered" children. Traditionally the Probation Service had produced reports in cases of disputed

custody, and supervised children on a Divorce Court Welfare Supervision Order. These functions were transferred to the Children and Family Court Advisory and Support Service (CAFCASS) – a move incidentally opposed by the judges in London, not just because of a loss of expertise, but because CAFCASS was considered unable to cope with the new influx of work. The net effect however was that the Probation Service was further removed from its court/social welfare roots. It meant too an additional drift towards a correctional rather than social work service, and of course the loss of trained personnel was simply another blow. One of the arguments for change however was beginning to appear regularly; that children, and parents should not be involved with a service more attuned to work with offenders. Or in the case of those requiring educational and social resources, these should more easily be accessed through other forms of social work. Another was that the Probation Service was not able to meet the complexity of the services required.

This loss was acutely felt by the service, and disliked by the courts especially the High Courts, but the loss was inevitable. The Probation Service was no longer equipped to offer a range of services for endangered children. The new service, CAFCASS, was created in Chapter II of Part I of the 2000 Act, and took over the Family Court work. CAFCASS is independent of the courts and Social Services but works under the rules of the Family Court. Its annual report (2015–6 HC 192) claims it is "the voice of the child in the family courts," offering services in public law, services to children in care proceedings, supervision applications by local authorities and private law involving custody and/or access. The complexity of the organisation and the range of services offered was unlikely to be matched by the existing Probation Service and the move towards CAFCASS was therefore inevitable.

5. Finally, victim contact work was extended. It is strange that the Probation Service had not allied itself with the victims of crime, one would have thought this would be a natural extension of its work and influence. The 2000 Act imposed duties on the newly created probation boards which involved the victim. Section 69 said that where an offender has been convicted of a sexual or

violent offence the local probation board must take reasonable steps to ascertain whether any appropriate person (the victim) wishes to make representation about whether the offender should be subject to any conditions or representation on his release, and if so what those requirements should be. The board is required to inform the victim of these conditions especially where they involve contact with the victim's family. Not an enormous change but a distinct one nonetheless, further pushing the Probation Service towards an offender based service.

There were other measures in the Act, namely those dealing with the increase in substance abuse. One was the introduction of the Drug Treatment and Testing Order (DTTO) based on the American drug court model. It was first mooted by Tony Blair when he was Shadow Home Secretary and introduced into the 2000 Act. It was a slimmed down version of the American model, and for that reason never likely to be effective.[37] Nor indeed was it. Similarly, there were proposals for all offenders in police stations to be drug tested. And again without proper controls and surveillance over those administering the tests and without clear guidelines as to the best way to deal with the results, they became a cosmetic exercise like the DTTO. Their relevance to the Probation Service was marginal insofar as the service was to supervise the DTTOs, but of course this was another example of Level 3 privatisation.

The next significant change came with the Carter Report in 2003. This report remains one of the most influential. It is also a classic example of neo liberalism, and provides much of the impetus to full privatisation. The dominating theme of the report was that certain public services could be delivered more effectively and cheaply through the introduction of the private and voluntary sectors. This of course was not new for to repeat and emphasise an earlier point; although privatisation was first suggested by a Conservative Government, New Labour simply continued that policy. So much so that towards the end of its period in office the Labour Government was signalling its wish to expand the use of competition based services. Unpaid work and victim contact services were identified as candidates. Later governments, including the Coalition Government, simply carried on where their predecessors left off. It is not therefore a question of a strategy determined according to a political hue, but of a dominating strategy that includes all.

Patrick Carter, later Lord Carter, a businessman, and said to be a friend of Jack Straw, was appointed as a Non Executive Director of HM Prison Service. He was commissioned to report on wider matters, particularly on the possibility of increasing measures of privatisation. His report was published in 2001 with later versions in 2003 and 2007.[38] Together they offer a coherent argument with the emphasis on what it called contestability – the use of competition to upgrade the quality of public services. The reports were accepted by government with surprising speed and many of the recommendations implemented under the 2007 Offender Management Act.

The 2001 report began with the observation that despite recent improvements a new approach was needed to break down the "silos of prison and probation" and ensure a better focus of managing offenders – "silos" was a term used a number of times throughout. The report said:

> The introduction of competition has provided a strong incentive for improvements in public providers ... driving down costs changing the culture and enabling flexible staffing structures to be introduced. ... Private providers need to be given an incentive to invest. ... Currently, there is minimal contestability in the probation service.
>
> *(p. 24)*

There were other comments which were highly significant such as,

> The system is dominated by two services ... which remain largely detached from each other.
>
> *(p. 23)*

Or,

> Prison and probation need to be focused on the management of the offender throughout their sentence. Effectiveness and value for

money can be further improved through greater use of competition from private and voluntary providers.

(p. 25)

Or again,

> Offender managers will provide end to end supervision. The offender manager will be the key part of the system ensuring offenders meet the conditions of their sentence and receive the help they need to reduce reoffending.
>
> *(p. 37)*

> The benefits of competition from the private and voluntary sectors could be extended further across both prison and probation.
>
> *(p. 4)*

> More effective service delivery can be achieved through greater contestability.
>
> *(p. 34)*

> The increased use of prison and probation since 1997 has been concentrated on first time offenders leading to poor use of additional investment.
>
> *(p. 3)*

It is easy and fashionable to criticise Carter for saying that he failed to understand the complexities of the criminal justice system, and that at a stroke he reduced 100 years of probation practice to the "juggernaut of neo liberalism"; Also, that his programme of reform was based on a few practices taken from the world of business; or that one of his major recommendations the merging of probation with the prison service has turned out to be a disaster for probation (see below). And it is correct to say there was nothing new in his report; that merging prison and probation had been suggested as far back as 1998,[39] and the introduction of the private sector in EM had already occurred. What was new was the coherence of the approach, the sheer audacity almost of suggesting a measure of competition in what had erstwhile been a service which thrived on cooperation. Yet consider some of Carter's critiques of existing practices. Take for example management within the Probation Service.

Carter saw better management as a key to a more efficient and effective service. Hitherto, management within the service was often patchy. In some places, notably Inner London up to the 1970s, it hardly existed – although subsequent Chief Probation Officers made considerable improvement in the latter years. Elsewhere, particularly in Nottingham, and under the leadership of the legendry Peter Pascall, it was different. There, a direct management structure was in operation with supervision of junior officers. Mostly, however, there was no management in the sense in which Carter saw management. There was a straightforward organisational structure with Probation Officer, Senior Probation Officer, Deputy Director, up to Chief Probation Officer, but there was little in this structure which was about management, and certainly not leadership. Basic grade Probation Officers worked as individual professionals; they were not managed in any real sense. Basic grade Probation Officers were left responsible for their decisions, not accountable to seniors. (Questions about what Senior Probation Officers do were regularly asked.) Hardly surprising then that Carter was concerned with the inefficiency of the service and wishing to provide "a better focus on managing offenders." Take for example this account of a young Probation Officer in the late 1960s who consulted his senior about a difficult case. After some discussion the senior made it clear whose responsibility it was and who should make the decision. "Whatever you decide you'd better get it right" was the senior's advice.

Management, or managerialism to use the modern term, is, according to Nellis and Gelsthorpe, the means by which the centre exerts detailed control over the periphery. If so then this is what the government intended; it wanted to reduce local autonomy and local practice. It wanted also to reduce costs. It saw the way forward as introducing a management structure, and altering the nature and sources of funding. Both followed from the precept of increasing effectiveness, and both were also difficult for the Probation Service or some outside commentators to accept. For example, critics such as Mike Nellis and Loraine Gelsthorpe saw some of the dangers of managerialism in the Probation Service which they believed would result in a "loss of humanity."[40]

Managerialism, they say, is about competition and market testing, about setting targets and performance indicators, about auditing and continuous improvement, and about contracting out privatisation. Where they see managerialism as full of dangers, and a means by which the Probation Service and its officers are reduced as professionals, Carter saw it as a means by which the Probation Service could reduce costs, become more efficient and drive up performance.

Nor was there much collaboration with other agencies. Carter said prison and probation needed to be focused on the management of offenders throughout their sentences. If some form of management existed it was described as "patchy," yet changes were clearly needed. Carter said it was vital that there was greater coherence between the work of the prison and Probation Services ensuring both prison and probation can work together. The solution? It came in two parts; first, Carter said that the Probation Service should be merged with the Prison Service, and second, there was to be "end to end management of offenders," who would be responsible for implementing a competition strategy. The expected results? Effectiveness and value for money would be improved through competition which will come from private and voluntary providers.

Or take another of Carter's criticisms that the Probation Service (and prisons) were dealing with too many low level offenders. Carter said "The increased use of prison and probation since 1997 has been concentrated on first time offenders leading to poor use of additional investment."[41] Again nothing new, but worth saying nonetheless. For decades the Probation Service had been taking too many offenders who were not only low risk but unlikely to reoffend. Rod Morgan comparing the decade up to 2003 concluded, as a result of his analysis of sentencing practices, that "offenders supervised by the Probation Service are clearly less serious in type" and that "more and more offenders are getting mired deeper and deeper into the criminal justice system for doing less."[42] Almost half of all offenders doing community service had no previous convictions.[43] The result, said Morgan, was that Probation Officers' caseloads were "silting up" with these low risk offenders.[44] The Probation Service itself was in part responsible for this "net widening," where a declining proportion of recommendations made in their court reports were for fines and discharges. The implication being that these offenders were ending up on probation or community service when they could have been otherwise dealt with.

Carter also wanted community sentences to be more demanding for medium risk offenders. Again, nothing new here, but there had always been a debate about the content of community sentences, and about whether offenders should (or should not) have to agree to be placed on the order. Carter's proposals raised suspicions that the government wanted to increase "the punitive element" of the community sentence. If he was he was simply stating what many in government had long since wanted; that community sentences should be more demanding, whether in time or effort.

Finally, the National Offender Management Service (NOMS) was introduced. This stemmed from Carter's assertion that "The system is dominated by two services ... which remain largely detached from each other."[45] NOMS was created in 2004. It became an executive agency and arose by combining parts of the Headquarters of the National Probation Service with HM Prison Service, together with some additional Home Office functions. It lasted until April 2017 when it was replaced by HM Prison and Probation Service (HMPPS). The original intention was to provide an overarching organisational structure that would deliver an end to end offender management, and manage the National Probation Service.[46]

The merger was not beneficial to the Probation Service. First there was the simple problem that the Prison Service was much larger than probation, which was outnumbered and out manoeuvred at every turn. Second the merger was a failure on grounds of policy. Julian Le Vay says Carter did not think through the merger.[47] NOMS was ill suited to adopt a commissioning model, it required a form of management that the Prison Service was unused to. Third, there were ideological difference which made the merger difficult. John Harding saw it as unwise; he accepted that probation was a law enforcement agency, but added that its conceptual roots lie in community justice.[48] He also thought the Probation Service could equally well have been merged with the police, or perhaps with others for within such an alliance a vast number of interactions are possible. Or again he said that whilst not denying the shared concern with the Prison Service for protecting the public from future harm through rigorous and credible forms of supervision, probation stands apart from the beliefs that support imprisonment. He thought the Probation Service was more at ease in understanding the community context in which crime takes place.

Finally, there were criticisms about the quality of NOMS management, especially the IT contracts, and by implication the manner in which it dragged the Probation Service down with it. The most trenchant criticisms came from the National Audit Office in 2009.[49] Briefly, in June 2004 NOMS initiated a National Offender Management System project (C-NOMIS) to implement a single offender management IT system across the Prison and Probation Services. It was due for completion by January 2008. By July 2007 NOMS had spent £155m, the project was two years behind schedule and estimated lifetime costs had risen to £690m. The Minister of State imposed a moratorium while options for reducing the project costs were sought.[50] The National Audit Office report said the project "had been hampered by poor management leading to a three year delay, a doubling in project costs and reductions in scope and benefits." It thought the problems could have been avoided if NOMS had established realistic budgets, timescales and governance for the project at the start, and followed basic project management principles. And for the future? "In delivering the new reduced programme NOMS needs to focus on better financial controls and more effective management." These were serious criticisms indeed, and of course the Probation Service was implicated by association.

In 2006 the Home Office produced a manifesto for contracting out certain aspects of probation work.[51] The fiscal crisis of 2008/9 later became a dominating influence, so that proposals which claimed to reduce costs as well as drive up quality were therefore welcomed. In September 2012 Chris Grayling arrived as Justice Secretary with a radical programme, *Transforming Rehabilitation*. Grayling's proposals fitted perfectly the Coalition Government's demands for a cost effective Probation Service. For the service itself they spelled disaster; and all that happened before was nothing as far as these new proposals were concerned. They were to produce the single most important change in the Probation Service's history.

The second period ended with the Carter Report and Grayling's appointment as Justice Secretary. The Probation Service had survived, only just. but the signs for the future were not good. Many commentators predicted the end was nigh, that the Probation Service would not survive, at least in its present form. Mike Nellis and Wing Hong Chui saw the managerial culture as the biggest threat to the service. In their view managerialism produced staff who were reduced to being minions, who merely followed procedures, who were technically informed, but insufficiently thoughtful, and who ended up with nothing ever consolidated.[52] Others such as NAPO saw the greatest risk in the purchaser/provider model which it said would eventually "split the service." Mair and Burke on the other hand were more optimistic; they saw survival as possible through the provision of community penalties. They thought there will always be a need for some type of community penalty, and they hoped the Probation Service would be able to undertake it.[53] What no one realised was that privatisation was but a short step away, and that it would mean the break-up of the Probation Service. It would mean a different service from anything that had been before, and to many commentators, policy makers, and politicians alike, it would all be a calamitous mistake. To others it was a necessary change brought on an inefficient service.

Stage three and privatisation and beyond

The final stage is from 2003 to 2014. This stage includes the 2007 Offender Management Act, the Government White Paper *Transforming Rehabilitation* and the subsequent legislation that introduced much of what we call the "privatisation of the Probation Service."

The legislation relating to the Carter report was delayed by the General Election. It appeared later mainly in the form of the 2007 Offender Management Act. This Act introduced many of Carter's proposals, much to the dismay of NAPO and the Probation Service generally. Section 1(1) of the Act sets out the new arrangements for the provision of what it calls "probation services," a term full of threat, as it implied something different from a traditional Probation "Service." The Section also required the Secretary of State to have regard to the aims of these Probation Services which are listed in Section 2(4) as being; the protection of the public, the reduction of offending, the proper punishment of offenders, ensuring offenders are aware of the effects of their crime, and the rehabilitation of offenders. No "advise, assist or befriend" here, but a hard statement of purpose setting the Probation Service within the full remit of criminal justice.

The Act gave the Secretary of State powers under Section 3(2) to make contractual or any other arrangements with any other person for the making of these probation provisions. Under this section, the Secretary of State has powers to contract with providers to deliver these services. Commissioning could be at a national, regional, and local level, but some low volume, high cost services could be commissioned on a national basis. This is an important section as it was the section used by Chris Grayling to change part of the Probation Service from public into private companies.

The Act also empowered probation boards to be transformed and transferred into 35 probation trusts. They were required to demonstrate levels of high performance in a number of areas, including the use of effective resources. Apparently, the government thought the earlier probation boards had stunted the growth of contestability, and of course Carter was eager to introduce that into the probation services. National Standards were further amended, with the Secretary of State required to publish them alongside the qualifications and experience or training required of staff working directly with offenders.

The result was a number of initiatives which followed Carter's vision of an efficient and effective service, well managed and with a mixture of public and private initiatives. The Guide to the Offender Management Act 2007 makes this clear: "We will be encouraging and offering incentives to all probation areas to apply "best value" principles in determining whether to deliver services in house or commission them from others."

Ken Clarke[54] opened up the debate in 2010 in a Green Paper saying the current rates of reoffending are unacceptable. Nearly half of adult offenders released from prison are reconvicted within a year. He also said that he was signalling an end to short term prison sentences saying it was virtually impossible to rehabilitate any inmate in less than 12 months. He said prisons were not effective in many cases. This could mean more offenders on community sentences, a further demonstration that community sentences were for punishment and the probation services' task was to enforce them.

The decision to end short term sentences was never taken, but the reconviction rate of these prisoners remained noticeably high. In December 2010 the first hint of what was to come can be found in plans to introduce Payment by Results (PbR), with a commitment to apply this system to all providers by 2015. This was followed by a consultation paper *Punishment and reform: effective probation services* and another called *Effective community sentences*. On the 9th January 2013 the government published *Summary of responses* to those earlier papers and also on that date published its key White Paper *Transforming Rehabilitation: a revolution in the way we manage offenders,* and in May 2013 the response, *Transforming Rehabilitation: a strategy for reform*.[55] The Offender Rehabilitation Bill was introduced to the House of Lords on the 9th May 2013, debated in both Houses and received the Royal Assent on the 13th February 2014. On the 1st February 2015 new providers began operating. It was all over in just a few years.

The White Paper *Transforming Rehabilitation* was promoted by Chris Grayling, the Lord Chancellor, who came to the post with a "history of privatisation." The White Paper contained a number of suggestions for change which included the abolition of the probation trusts, contracting out the majority of probation work to private and voluntary sector providers in 21 new Community Rehabilitation Companies (CRCs) introducing a new National Probation Service (NPS) to manage high risk offenders, and new ways to deal with breaches. New statutory rehabilitation programmes would also be introduced whereby all offenders sentenced to less than 12 months imprisonment were to be supervised. A "Through The Gate" service was also to be introduced whereby offenders were offered a resettlement service in custody and before release, and be transferred to resettlement prisons in the last part of their sentence. The government would introduce PbR to develop more effective ways of rehabilitating offenders, and rewarding providers. PbR, would it was claimed, open up the market to a diverse range of providers, and develop and use an integrated offender management method to better manage offenders by getting partner agencies to work together.

The Bill was introduced to the House of Lords on the 20th May 2013. The Second Reading debate was introduced by Lord McNally (Col 633) who said that the purpose of the Bill was to break the cycle of reoffending. He said that in 2012 there were 600,000 crimes committed by people who had broken the law previously. Almost half the offenders were released from prisons within the year, that is to say 58% of those sentenced to prison for terms of less than 12 months. And yet, said Lord McNally, there is no statutory requirement for most of this group to receive supervision and support. As a result many leave the prison gates with little more than £46.00 and no other forms of aftercare. A greater proportion of women than men in custody are serving sentences of 12 months or less – 21% compared with 10% of men in 2011 – and many of those women were victims of domestic violence. The aim of the Bill, said Lord McNally, was to transform the support available for offenders given a short prison sentence by introducing a 12 month period of rehabilitation in the community after release.

There was general support for the Bill, although some doubts were raised about the prospects of making savings by opening up the services to private providers, and there were other doubts about the possibility of giving such large numbers of offenders support, but generally speaking there was support. Surprisingly so, as there was to be no extra money available; the expectation was that the money for extra services would come from savings. Lord Ramsbotham was one of the few critics. He was unimpressed. "When has legislation ever been able to guarantee the consistent availability, provision and affordability of the money and people required to produce that support?" (Col 661). And on cost Lord Ramsbotham asked,

> What factors did the Government consider in estimating that there might be additional costs of only £5m a year? What is the Government's estimate of the cost of providing a rehabilitative service to offenders released from custodial sentences of less than 12 months and how much are they looking to recover through competition?

In fact no such costings had been made. Lord Ramsbotham was also concerned about the timetable, believing the procedure to be rushed. He thought the government should have taken more time, prepared a pilot, and considered other options. Deliberately misquoting Caliban's speech in *The Tempest*, Lord Ramsbothan said the Bill was full of "Soundbites and hot air that give hurt and delight not" (Col 654). Lord

Woolf, another critic, thought the programme might produce the opposite effect to that intended; that it might increase the number of short sentenced prisoners because the courts would see the legislation as offering assistance to those most in need. He also asked whether every prisoner required such an elaborate expensive rehabilitative process: "Remember that 42% do not reoffend. Who will judge whether this case or that one needs to be the subject of the action?" Finally, Lord Woolf made the point that alternatives were available; the Liverpool Community Court, one of the newly introduced Problem Solving Courts, was in need of funding, and already offering some measure of success. Why not direct attention there?[56]

Requests to delay were not accepted and the programme formally began in late 2013, when the Minister of Justice invited bids to run the CRCs. Thirty bidders were shortlisted, eight were chosen, although these eight bidders could subcontract to other organisations. In June 2014 the 21 CRCs were created. Staff employed by probation trusts were divided into two groups, some to the NPS, others to the CRCs. On the 1st February 2015 the eight new providers took ownership.

The White Paper was followed by the Offender Rehabilitation Act 2014. That Act was "to make provision about the release of offenders, to make provision about the extension period for extended sentence prisoners, to make provision about community orders and suspended sentence orders and for connected purposes." It received the Royal Assent on 13 March 2014. The CRCs were created under an earlier Act, the Offender Management Act 2007, and not therefore under the later Offender Rehabilitation Act 2014. Under Section 3 of the 2007 Act, the Secretary of State had powers to make contractual or other arrangements with any other person for the making of probation provision.

Thus began the Probation Service's period of privatisation. It began amid controversy, with few in the Probation Service having little hope for the future. Critics of the Justice Secretary said he failed to seek or heed advice, and introduced it with undue haste. The Shadow Justice Spokesman in the House of Lords debate thought this owed more to ideology than criminology – a persistent criticism of the Justice Secretary.[57]

The Justice Secretary was also accused of failing to pilot the project. There remains some dispute about this, and whether any piloting was undertaken. In May 2012 the Ministry of Justice tended contracts for a pilot offender programme in Leeds Prison, but it closed the competition after bidders decided not to compete. They said they could not manage such a level of financial risk.[58] There were pilot schemes in two prisons, Peterborough and Doncaster, but they were concerned primarily with PbR (discussed below) and not about the separation of services. They were also concerned with supervision on release but as they were only for voluntary after care, not those on licence they could not be called "pilot" studies in the strict sense of the term.

Another area of dispute concerned the Risk Register. In 2013 a Risk Register had been completed, but the Justice Secretary refused to publish it,[59] and anyway it was conducted after the privatisation programme had been introduced. This brought forth another scathing comment from Lord Ramsbotham who said in the House of Lords debates:

> During my professional career I have been involved in a number of change programmes ... including having to reduce the size of the Army ... but never before have I come across a detailed assessment of risks being drafted only after a plan has been agreed and announced let alone began its passage through Parliament.[60]

The Strategic Risk Assessment provided to peers before the House of Lords Debates sets out the levels of risks for certain aspects of the programme, described by Lord Ramsbotham as "the most damning indictment of an imperfectly considered initiative as he has ever seen."[61] For example, the government accepted that there were sufficiently high risks that the programme could not mitigate according to its timetable and the timescales it set. There were also high risks that the services would not meet, which it said would lead to operational failure and loss of public confidence. And there were other high risks likely to come from legal challenges that would result in a failure to deliver the programme on time. Yet the government did little to try to reduce these risks, let alone try to overcome them.

The highest risks were reserved for those areas associated with the costs of the programme and the likely savings, or in government's terms what it called "value for money." A persistent theme throughout has been the failure of government to provide an adequate system of costs and savings for this project, a point which will be picked up again in a later chapter on PbR. In the Strategic Risk Assessment the highest risk was given to what was called "affordability objectives." It said "the reforms cannot be demonstrated or met leading to failure to secure approvals during the programme or financial and operational risk and reputational damage to the department after implementation." The risk levels were such as to be classified as having a "significant detrimental effect on the programme." That risk of a "detrimental effect" was in some cases as high as 80%.

There were many other risks, a total of 17 listed altogether, some in high risk categories others less so – one in the lower group was "that the programme does not deliver on time" and one slightly higher listed as "there is a risk that the new service and market models implemented as a result of the programme are ineffective and/or inefficient leading to operational financial and reputational impacts and failure to realise the planned benefits of the reforms."

The so-called "Risk Causes" are themselves interesting. Take for example that relating to "… rolling out Payment by Results by 2015." The Impact Rating was at the highest level (at 5) and the "likelihood of it occurring" at over 80%. The "Risk Causes" were listed as: "Failure to align ministerial expectations"; "complexity scale and pace of the programme"; as well as "failure to align the programme with public commitment on Payment by Results." Or take the one on "failing to secure approvals." The Impact Level is again at the highest level with the "likelihood" slightly reduced at between 51% and 80%, but still high nonetheless. It is extraordinary that any government should go ahead with a programme of such complexity with so much left outstanding, and with such high levels of risk in such sensitive areas.)

Finally, there was criticism about the failure on the part of the Justice Secretary to produce costings for the project. The failure is particularly odd because a major justification for the privatisation programme had always been that it was a cost saving exercise. Yet we find little attention given to cost, although one would have expected that certain basic costings would have been undertaken and published before the programme was introduced. The House of Commons Justice Committee, which reported in January 2014,[62] thought so too. It accepted that the ultimate goal of the programme was to reduce offending and reduce cost. However it said the Ministry has been less than forthcoming over the costs of the programme.[63] The Committee noted that there was an "absence of published projections of the likely reductions in reoffending, or estimates of how this might impact on the future costs of the system." Accordingly, "it is not possible to predict whether savings will be swallowed up by increased demand on the prison system" or by reduced funding of existing services, or by other funders.[64] In reply the Ministry of Justice said it was not prepared to make public many of the costs as they are "commercially sensitive" and disclosure would "prejudice negotiations with potential providers."[65] The Justice Committee were also concerned whether there was sufficient funding in place to meet the costs of the new system.[66] No information was given to meet these concerns.

To introduce a service on the basis that costs will be recovered, and in the hope that all things will turn out right in the end, seems unusual to say the least. One would have expected that certain basic costs would have been announced, such as the savings expected to come from the programme, and the costs of running the newly formed National Probation Service. These are not "commercially sensitive." The funds made available for the CRCs, and the costs of increased caseloads for the CRCs concerning their increased involvement in prison after care may well be, but this is not only private money that is involved here. At some future stage this information should be made public, but there has been no sign that it will be. Quite the reverse; the government seems intent on keeping it secret.

Some information on costs can be quarried from various publications. For example the Ministry of Justice in 2013[67] gave estimates of £25m being the extra cost of breach of requirements of orders from offenders discharged from prison, and a further £25m being the estimated costs associated with other aspects of breach proceedings, i.e. police time etc. There were other costs from rehabilitation services for those offenders dependant on drugs, but the Ministry said it could not quantify these. There were also costs from providing rehabilitative services but these too could not be quantified, and were dependant on what was called the value of competition. There were said to be no significant costs arising from community services and with the increased flexibility in the delivery of community orders (including suspended sentences) it was expected there would be savings due to reduced offending. No figures were given on this either, as the Ministry of Justice said "We have not quantified these benefits, as we cannot predict the success rate of the providers."[68]

One would have expected something more detailed than this. It was later feared that numerous other costs would be incurred as a result of privatisation; for example, the costs of new IT services, the costs of redundancy payments to existing staff, and the extra costs of managing relations between the NPS and CRCs. These too need to be quantified and set out with the others. Set against these are the expected savings which the government say will occur, but again, it gives no figures to support this contention. The whole exercise relating to the costs of the programme has been less than satisfactory; either the costings have never been undertaken it which case the programme should have been deferred or they have been undertaken but kept from public scrutiny, in which case the government has failed to keep the public informed.

What was referred to as "undue haste" was the speed with which the whole programme was introduced and finally passed into law. By modern standards it was certainly quick, and if not "undue" then it was certainly "hasty." It was all over in less than two years. The Shadow Justice Secretary hoped there was still time for Ministers to admit this is all a terrible mistake and abandon what it called this reckless privatisation. No such admission or abandonment occurred. Nor did it seem that the government was affected by the adverse publicity. Headlines talked of "Probation officers feeling betrayed" or "The profit motives being introduced with rehabilitative techniques," and "Death of the probation ideal."[69] None of which appeared to have any impact on the government.

The period following privatisation is dealt with in the subsequent chapters. Here I only want to point out that numerous reports and assessments have been made, one such summary of events coming from David Lidington, the newly appointed Justice Secretary who in 2017 admitted the Probation Service was "falling short of expectations." He said measures designed to support prisoners on release "did not command the confidence of the Courts."[70] Earlier, in 2016 the Public Accounts Committee made similar comments.[71] It said the committee found "a mixed practice"[72] with a "lack of experienced management staff is of concern." It reserved most of their criticisms for "Through The Gate" services, where it said over two thirds of offenders released from prison had not received enough help in relation to accommodation, employment, or finance.[73] Its general conclusion was that the new arrangements were not yet stable. Another criticism is from the first Annual Report of HM Inspectorate of Probation[74] (December 2017) showing how the government's *Transforming Rehabilitation* was working. The general conclusion was equally critical; results show that early teething problems have largely been resolved but more deep seated problems prevail.[75]

In the following chapters I want to look more closely at some of these "deep seated problems" and do so by describing in detail the main features of privatisation as it applies to the Probation Service. *Transforming Rehabilitation* has attracted considerable interest and attention the most important being from that report by HM Probation Inspectorate in December 2017, and a later House of Commons Justice Committee which met in January 2018 and again in July 2018. Finally, for these purposes there is the Government publication *Strengthening probation, building confidence*[76] which acknowledges some of the failings of the privatised system. Details of this will be considered later, but its main aim is to try to rescue some of the more damaging features of *Transforming Rehabilitation*, especially those concerning the private companies. So, what started as a few minor changes to the Probation Service in the 1960s has ended with a privatised service and a barrage of criticisms alongside a narrative which has still a long way to go.

Notes

1 See for example Bean P T (1976) *Rehabilitation and deviance* (Routledge) which is an attack on that earlier form of rehabilitation. One solution offered was the "Non treatment paradigm for probation practice" suggested by Tony Bottoms and Bill McWilliams (1979) in the *British Journal of Social Work*. Vol. 9, pp. 159–202. This proposed practical help rather than treatment.
2 Hood R and Sparks R (1971) *Key issues in criminology*. Weidenfeld and Nicolson. Pp. 188–189.
3 My own caseload at the time in Marylebone Magistrates Court, Inner London was over 100, including some on Broadmoor licence, many on Preventative Detention After Care (as it was at the time) with the usual mixture of serious and non serious offenders, but all with a multitude of

Government intervention 63

problems. What did "success" mean for this group of offenders? No one seemed to know.
4 See Mair G and Burke L (2012) *Redemption, rehabilitation and risk management* for a more detailed description of this and subsequent periods where the Probation Service was under attack.
5 There are two references to Barbara Wootton's discussion on Community Service. The first in 1973 entitled "Community service" published in the *Criminal Law Review*, pp. 16–22, and the second in 1977, "Some reflections on the first five years of Community Service" in *Probation Journal* Vol. 24, No. 4, pp. 110–112.
6 Mair G (2004) The origins of "What Works" in England and Wales: a house built on sand. In Mair G (ed) *What matters in probation*. Willan Publishing pp. 12–33.
7 Wootton B (1973) op. cit p. 22.
8 Home Office (1984) Statement of National Objectives and Priorities Stationary Office. It was introduced into the House of Commons on 1st May 1984 by Leon Brittan (Vol. 59, Col. 125–6) who said SNOP was intended to provide a basis for a more systematic approach to the management and deployment of resources. He said he expected it would command a large measure of support from the Probation Service.
9 Lord Harris, House of Lords Debate. The Probation Service. Objectives and Practice. 16 May 1984, Cols. 1477–1500.
10 Ibid.
11 BBC Radio 4: File on Four. 18th February 2013.
12 Home Office. (1988) *Punishment, custody and the community*. HMSO. Cmnd 424.
13 It was The Wolds, which opened in 1992.
14 Nellis M (2004) Electronic Monitoring and the community supervision of offenders. In Bottoms A, Rex S and Robertson G (eds) *Alternatives to prison*. Willan Publishing. pp. 224–257
15 Ibid. Pg. 229.
16 Ibid. Pg. 247
17 Ibid. Pg. 249.
18 Ibid. Pg. 249 and 253–254.
19 Nellis M (2004). op. cit.
20 For a discussion on the cost of Probation see Mair G and Burke L (2012) op. cit. Pg. 148.
21 Labour Party (1997) Manifesto: Britain will be better with New Labour. The Labour Party. Pg. 3–5. See also Whitehead P (2010) *Exploring modern probation*. Policy Press.
22 Home Office (1995) *Strengthening punishment in the community: a consultation document*. (March) HMSO. Cm 2780.
23 See Mair G and Burke L (2012) op. cit., pg. 153–157 for a discussion on the position of probation during this period.
24 Rumgay J (2004) The barking dog? Partnerships and effective practice. In Mair G (ed) *What matters in probation*. Willan Publishing, pp. 122–145.

25 Dominey J (2012) A mixed market for probation services; can lessons from the recent past help the future? *Probation Journal*. Vol. 59, No. 4, pp. 339–354. See particularly pages 341–342.
26 Martinson R (1974) What Works? Questions and answers about prison reform. *The Public Interest*. Vol. 35, No. 5, pp. 22–54. See also Chui W (2003) "What Works" in reducing offending. Principles and programmes. In Chui W and Nellis M (eds) *Moving probation forward*. Pearson Longman. pp. 56–73.
27 Ibid. Pg. 24.
28 Mair G and Burke L. (2012) op. cit. Pg. 159.
29 Ibid. Pg. 120.
30 Ibid. Pg. 159.
31 Ibid. Ch. 8.
32 Mair G (2004) op. cit. Pg. 16.
33 Mair G and Burke L (2012) op. cit. Pg. 163–169.
34 Ibid. Pg. 164.
35 Ibid. Pg. 20.
36 Ibid. Pg. 21.
37 See Bean P T (2014) *Drugs and crime* (4th Edition) (Routledge) for a discussion on American Drug Courts.
38 Carter P (2003) *Managing offenders reducing crime*. Strategy Unit. This report was directed towards a review of correctional services and in a way predated the privatisation of probation. It also suggested that probation and prison were dealing with far too many low level offenders. Thus diversion from probation was to be encouraged.
39 In a White Paper from the Home Office in 1998 entitled "Joining forces to protect the public. Prisons probation. A consultation document." Stationery Office.
40 Nellis M and Gelsthorpe L (2003) Human rights and the probation values debate. In Chui W and Nellis M (eds) *Moving probation forward*. Pearson Longman. pp. 227–224.
41 Carter (2003) op. cit. Pg. 3.
42 Morgan R (2003) Thinking about the demand for probation services. *Probation Journal*. Vol. 50, No. 1, pp 7–19. Pg. 15.
43 Ibid. Pg. 16.
44 Ibid. Pg. 15.
45 Carter (2003) op. cit. Pg. 23.
46 Carr N (2017) Goodbye NOMS. Where to next? *Probation Journal*. Vol. 64, No. 2, pp. 91–93.
47 Le Vay J (2016) *Competition for prisons*. Policy Press.
48 Harding J (1999) The probation service in the 20th century. *Criminal Justice Matters*. No. 38, p. 28.
49 House of Commons. National Audit Office (2009) *National offender management information system*. The Stationary Office. (June 37).
50 Ibid. Para 4.
51 Home Office (2006) *A five year strategy for protecting the public and reducing offending*. Home Office. (Cm 6717).

52 Chui W and Nellis M (2003) op. cit. Pg. 224.
53 Mair G and Burke L (2012) op. cit. Pg. 192.
54 In a Green Paper, Ministry of Justice (2010) *Breaking the cycle: effective punishment, rehabilitation and sentencing of offenders.* (Cm 7972).
55 There were 5 major Government Publications relating to this matter. They were (2012) *Punishment and reform: effective probation services.* (CP (R) 7/2012) (March); A second in 2012 *Punishment and reform: effective community sentences* (CP 7/2012). Then in May 2013 *Punishment and reform: Summary of Responses*. The fourth by the Ministry of Justice in 2003 *Transforming Rehabilitation: a revolution in the way we manage offenders.* (CP 1/2013) and finally also in 2013 Transforming Rehabilitation: a strategy for reform. (Cm 8619). (CPR 16/2013).
56 House of Lords Debates (2013) Second Reading. Cols. 633–661.
57 NAPO (2014) *Transforming Rehabilitation and the impact on crime reduction reoffending and probation resources.* (September).
58 Ministry of Justice (2016) Transforming Rehabilitation. The Nation Audit Office Report. Para. 1.17.
59 These quotes are from NAPO Briefing Papers numbers 249, 252, and 254.
60 Quoted in NAPO Issue 249.
61 Lord Ramsbotham. Pers. Com.
62 House of Commons (2014) Crime reduction policies: a coordinated approach? Interim report of the government's Transforming Rehabilitation programme. HC 1004.
63 Ibid. Para 30.
64 Ibid. Para 35.
65 Ibid. Paras 29–30.
66 Ibid. Para 34.
67 Ministry of Justice (2013) Impact assessment of the Offender Management Bill. (May). This impact assessment gives a summary of some of the costs of providing a privatised service and the likely impact on other agencies.
68 Ibid. Para 33.
69 Headlines quoted by Dent I on Politics.co.uk in 2014.
70 *The Times* (22nd April 2017) .
71 House of Commons Public Accounts Committee (2016) (September) Transforming Rehabilitation. HC 484. Pg. 6.
72 Ibid. Para. 2.
73 Ibid. Para 26.
74 HM Inspectorate of Probation for England and Wales (2017) *Annual Report* 2017.
75 Ibid. Pg. 5.
76 Ministry of Justice (2018) *Strengthening probation, building confidence*, Cm 9613.

3

THE PROBATION SERVICE'S RESPONSE

In his assessment of the Probation Service George Mair thought that probation always believed it was on the side of the angels and that its staff were "the good guys" of the criminal justice system. He said that meant it tended to be somewhat complacent. He also thought that a good deal of research has been complicit in this, so that criminologists, for example, have never subjected probation to the same levels of critique that the police, prison officers, or sentencers have had to face.[1] The implication being that this form of protection, akin to political correctness, had done the Probation Service no favours. Rather, he thought it had been damaging, leaving the service without the ability to help itself in the battle to survive.

There is something to be said in favour of Mair's critique. There are numerous examples where the Probation Service has seen itself as "on the side of the angels," believing it was operating for the best in an otherwise uncertain world. Or if not, then wanting to stand aloof from some of the more morally unattractive, yet realistic features of the criminal justice system. It never sought collaboration with the Prison or Police Service, seeing the former as "punitive" and the latter as "authoritarian," and in doing so held a lofty detachment from them. Criminologists have helped foster the image of a self-righteous organisation, and if not actively promoting it, then at least not challenging or attacking it. The result, according to Mair, is a service built on "shaky foundations" leading to what he calls "a narrative of loss."[2]

Whatever changes may have occurred and however unpleasant they must have seemed, no one could deny that the Probation Service was warned. There were numerous events and government pronouncements, giving clear signals of what was to come, but the service's response was not always appropriate. It seemed not to understand what was being asked of it. Sometimes it gave a grudging response to government proposals, others it simply ignored and to others it was downright hostile. An example of the former was the introduction of Community Service in 1973. This was an obvious challenge to existing practice, but generally welcomed throughout the criminal justice system, except by the Probation Service, who initially opposed it. Eventually it gave Community Service grudging acceptance. By then the opportunity was missed, and by not appearing constructive, the service was left with the reputation of being reactionary and self-serving.

With hindsight events have unfolded in a clear trajectory towards some form of privatisation. It is unlikely the service could have prevented this, but it may have influenced events, and if not have prevented privatisation then at least it might have changed its course. In this chapter I want to look at some key events at which it failed to act convincingly, or failed to appreciate changes taking place in government circles. But before doing so, I want to highlight the point that it began at a serious disadvantage. That is to say in any clash, dispute, or quarrel with the government, the service could not compare with the strength of the Prison Service or the police. Being one of the smallest, if not the smallest in the criminal justice system, it was vulnerable. As such it became easy to control, and in times of austerity the easiest to use as a template for dealing with government excess.

Representing the service

Of equal importance however was the governance of the service. For the service to be protected its governance needed to be framed in such a way as to be able to promote and develop it. That means it needed to have influence, which in practical terms meant having direct access to government and being represented at the highest level. Yet prior to privatisation there was no such facility, at least in the key years surrounding the Carter Report and immediately thereafter. At the point when the National Probation Service was formed in 2001, there was no one with influence, and no one to represent the Probation Service at the upper echelons of government, especially the Home Office. That is to say there was no one to brief ministers about issues affecting the service, and no one to see the wider picture, or represent the service and its views. Had there been an organisation such as the Probation Reform Trust, as there was a Prison Reform Trust, this might have helped. A director general at its head could have represented the service, whether to government, or to a wider public.

Prior to privatisation the governance of the service was such as to make it easy for government to make decisions about the Probation Service without much need for consultation. For many years the service was organised into small local probation areas. These may have been ideal as local organisations with local representation, but they had little impact or influence on government policy. Later when they were organised into trusts they were larger, but still not large enough to be effective. This fragmentation of the service was a serious drawback when it came to influencing events and protecting itself against the type of proposal offered under *Transforming Rehabilitation*.

There was more formal contact with ministers after the National Probation Service was formed, and the appointment of Ethnie Wallace as head of that service. She seems to have had some impact, yet was in office for only a short time. The new appointees lasted until the service was merged with the Prison Service to form the National Offender Management Service (NOMS). Once that happened its fate was clear. The merger into NOMS in 2004 almost obliterated the Probation Service. Whatever the justifications for the merger, the Probation Service was overwhelmed by another service more in tune with and more able to understand and work with the current political climate than its smaller neighbour. It was said that a visitor to NOMS would see NOMS as resembling a prison landing; all the talk was of prisons, there was nothing about probation. By the time the merger had taken place much of the damage had been done, and the Probation Service already selected for change.

The other possibility, that is the Probation Service could have been be merged with police, appears not to have been considered. Yet the Probation Service had much in common with the police: both were community based services, and both had worked together in the past. Both were concerned with the plight of the victims, and both operated within the setting of the courts. Carter however was more interested in establishing an organisation which he said would "provide end to end management of offenders."[3] He wanted prison and probation to work together, not probation and police.

Nor were there committees within the service able to act as its representative. The Association of Chief Officers of Probation (ACOP) was its major representative organisation outside of NAPO, its trade union. ACOP was formed in the mid-1980s, disbanded in 2001, and its name later changed to the Probation Chiefs Association (PCA). That organisation ceased to exist after the National Probation Service was formed, so that when *Transforming Rehabilitation* was introduced there was not even ACOP to represent it. And anyway, ACOP had no negotiating powers, nor does it appear it had much influence. It is hard to point to any changes in policy and practice as a result of proposals from ACOP. Its influence generally was benign but hardly influential. Lol Burke is critical of ACOP or PCA, and he includes in this the National Association of Probation Officers, the officers' trade union (NAPO), all of whom he says held probation dear, but were not always unified in their opposition to government control.[4] That ACOP had such limited influence is a further reminder that the Probation Service was not represented where it mattered.

There is no doubt its trade union, NAPO, has been consistent in its opposition to privatisation, and has vigorously represented the service, but whether this has always been of benefit is a different matter. NAPO has kept up a consistent barrage of criticism but again whether it has been influential or produced any deserved changes is difficult to say. It opposed privatisation from the outset, and four years later in its "News Line" (on June 16th 2017) still thundered out the same message. "*Transforming Rehabilitation* has proved calamitous and needs to be unpicked and addressed urgently ...." It saw the CRCs as "a recipe for disaster" posing "a massive risk to public safety," they being, "untried, untested and in our view ideologically flawed."[5] In contrast ACOP offered a more conciliatory approach, but as things turned out was no more successful.

However sometimes a little less confrontation from NAPO could perhaps have been more effective. A less direct political approach might also have helped, suggesting more collaboration and offering more unity. For example, the reaction of NAPO during the miners' strike in 1985 had a damaging effect on future relationships with the government. It sowed seeds of distrust that lasted for years. NAPO, at its AGM, passed a resolution calling on members to refuse to undertake Social Enquiry Reports on offenders charged under the Emergency Powers Act 1974. This was clear evidence that Probation Officers, through their trade union representatives, were allowing political considerations to influence their decisions. They were seeking to distinguish between those actions that were seen as "criminal proper" and others "prompted by political motives," which in NAPOs terms only co incidentally infringed the law.

This was an example where NAPO has not always served the Probation Service well. Michael Day in his commentary on NAPO said that in any union it is the more extreme and articulate who grab public attention and force issues, implying that in this instance the extremists prevailed.[6] He added that union debates encourage the rhetoric of extremism and over simplification.[7] That may be so, but governments of whatever political hue take notice of such activities, seeing them as challenges to their authority. And in times of austerity they will be less sympathetic. Michael Day's conclusion was that NAPO's reaction to the miner's strike ended up pleasing nobody. NAPO was dismissed by the Left as part of the system, and by the Right as part of the problem.[8] John Budd and Tony Knivett, erstwhile senior figures in the Probation Service, also take NAPO to task. They suggest NAPO should be reformed to become more dedicated to welfare, pay, and conditions, and the representation of staff facing disciplinary procedures, i.e. act as a traditional trade union, and be less concerned with pursuing a political agenda or ideological interpretations of society and offending.[9]

There is no doubt NAPO had limitations. Often it failed to see the implications of what was being offered and opposed changes in an almost Luddite way. For example, in a Briefing Paper in February 2011 it stated, "All initiatives involving the private sector and the probation service in recent years have been problematic or have failed."[10] It then gave a list of such failures including forms of Levels 1 and 2 privatisation. These included the provision of beds in bail hostels to Clear Springs, a company with no previous experience in criminal justice. This company failed to control anti-social behaviour in the hostels alongside a catalogue of further crimes, all said to be due to a lack of supervision. NAPO then listed failures in catering, cleaning, and other facilities which were privatised, including what it called "disastrous IT failures" where the projects were abandoned leading to losses of millions of pounds. It was right for NAPO to draw attention to them, but it did so through a political message where the aim was to oppose all forms of privatisation, including that of Levels 2 and 3. It said at the end of the Briefing Paper, that, "Arguably the motive of the private sector would be to make profits for their shareholders and not protect the public and communities."[11] A little less political stridency might have had greater effect.

In one sense, of course, NAPO was doing no more than representing the bulk of the Probation Service's views about privatisation. The Probation Service was always suspicious of proposals for private sector involvement. When work began to be contracted out, as with the introduction of Community Service, the Probation Service saw this as an unwelcome intrusion. It feared job losses, and feared too that the service would lose its position as a monopoly provider for work with offenders in the community. Later, when NAPO also actively opposed these proposals, this merely confirmed that the Probation Service was unwilling to accept and embrace change. Dividing lines were being established; neo liberalism on one side, and traditional ways of working on the other.

Training and selection

Throughout the 1960s and beyond there was discussion within the Probation Service about its identity and its aspirations to be a professional organisation. The aim was to be akin to traditional professions such as law and medicine. In numerous respects it failed, but none more so than in the training and selection of its members. For a number of years, certainly up to 1997, there was no single training programme, and this severely weakened the service. There were three routes of entry into the service; for those under the age of 30, who were expected to undertake a full time two-year university course leading to a diploma in social studies (or the like), but if a graduate this was reduced to one year. This was followed by a one-year training programme comprising two practical placements interspersed with a three month theoretical course at Rainer House. If over aged 30, then only the one year "Rainer House course" applied. But there were also the so called "direct entrants," where no training at all was given – from 1946 to 1961 about one in four of the service were direct entrants.[12] During this period the Home Office was responsible for selection and training. Later, it largely abandoned that responsibility.

In 1997 Jack Straw introduced the Diploma in Probation Studies, the nub of it being that training involved spending half the time in practice and the other half in a university – although this could involve distance learning. These training courses were in existence, about 10 years before they were replaced by the current system. Now (2018) there are two routes to training. One is as before, which is a fast track degree course for graduates with relevant degrees, the other an incremental route involving periods of full time practice with a build up of academic credit.

Prior to this, for those undertaking university courses responsibility for selection was handed to those running the university courses. The qualification offered was invariably an MA in Social Work or perhaps a Certificate in Social Work (CQSW) qualification. Too often probation was an adjunct to the main course, and where recognised then often of lesser importance than the demands of Social Work. These qualifications reflected what was being taught and the practical placements provided: the emphasis was on social work methods, and social work practice. Probation was relegated to these demands. It meant Probation Officers were poorly trained in probation, but highly trained in social work, the real problem being that the difference was never considered. Good social workers were thought to be good Probation Officers and vice versa. Moreover, students on the courses, especially courses offering post graduate degrees, were selected on their social work potential, not on whether they would make good Probation Officers. That meant the Probation Officers accountability to the courts and the state was not always considered, nor was the primary aim to reduce criminality.

In spite of recent changes to the training programme there are still numerous criticisms of the existing system. One criticism is that it does not stretch the candidates intellectually, another is that having lost its social work roots, the training programmes have not been able to promote new ones. Smith says that although the core curriculum is now more focussed on criminology, there remain elements of continuity with the old versions of social work. This is not because those who deliver the programme are reluctant to adapt to new thinking, but because of the "incoherence of official thinking on probation."[13] It is a familiar accusation; training has never been seriously thought through, leaving it open to different interpretations.

This incoherence, perhaps call it muddled thinking, has not helped the service. Again, compare the police or prison service where there was always more certainty about outcome and approach. In Probation there was never a clear statement of purpose understandable to the public, or a clarity of purpose which reflected what government and public want and need. Fragmentation in training is part of a wider more pervasive form of structural fragmentation that has beset the service. Had there been an Institute of Probation, as there now is, responsible for selection, recruitment and training, there might have been a greater measure of coherence in the training programmes, and a greater measure of control than has existed hitherto. It was clearly a mistake to allow training to be under the control of Universities, merged with and part of a wider social work programme with different standards of recruitment, different course structures and different qualifications at the end of the course. What that produced was a system dominated by social work thinking, with disparate systems of approach. Moreover no two courses were alike. An Institute could have avoided most of these problems by setting standards and conditions of service, that is to say producing a standardised curriculum covering all what was being taught, and demanding certain requirements whether of entrance, or quality of course. It might even have commissioned or promoted research.

One of the early strengths of the service was that it attracted mature entrants, sometimes called second careerists. This group was reduced in numbers as the Universities increased their influence on training. This, to the dismay of those who saw these second careerists as bringing additional stability to the service. John Budd and Tony Knivett[14] say selection should focus on this group who are also motivated by public service as they bring to the service an extra level of maturity. Their argument is, a future Probation Service should encourage this group, who have much to offer and who would help provide strength to a future service.

Probation as social work

The link with social work was both its strength and weakness. It was a strength because it helped promote that "island of decency," so respected by probation supporters. Its weakness was it created confusion about the task in hand. When the new training programme was introduced – i.e. the Diploma in Probation Studies – it was fiercely resisted by some members of the Probation Service because it illustrated that the ties with social work were being loosened. It meant probation was being pushed further into adopting a crime reduction perspective, and this was seen to be to the detriment of social work practice. The fear was that criminology was to become more important than social work studies.

Yet it was difficult to know what it meant to be a social worker as Probation Officer. Presumably, it was about providing a social work service for the courts, but Probation Officers clearly did more than this, and anyway what does a "social work service" do in the criminal justice system? Is it on the side of the victim, or the offender? That was never clear. Social workers and Probation Officers for many years shared the same training courses, usually with a nodding acceptance that probation was different, but being together helped produce the assertion that probation was social work. Yet it clearly was not. Social work is about enhancing social functioning and overall well being, probation is about preventing the commission of further offences. There may be a social work input in the process of crime reduction, and that input may help towards the overall goal, but the aims are different. John Budd and Tony Knivett say probation is about acquiring the skills and knowledge required to carry out the range of probation duties, which may involve correctional therapeutic methods which are to be combined with authority.[15] Social work is about something quite different.

Linking probation to social work did not provide the governments with what they wanted. Governments wanted to reduce crime, reduce costs, and enhance public protection. Crime is expensive, and prison additionally so. The task of probation therefore was to provide a crime reduction service in the community, and in doing so demonstrate its worth. Claiming to be social workers was unlikely to convince governments that it was committed to that crime reduction programme, except perhaps by coincidence. Unsurprisingly, governments, of whatever political hue, demanded it move in their direction, for it was the government after all that was doing the funding.

One unfortunate outcome of the links with social work was that a form of political extremism developed in a number of social work courses of the late 1970s and 1980s. It became fashionable for some students to adopt a Marxist perspective which was fostered by the publication of a book by Hilary Walker and Bill Beaumont entitled *Probation work: critical theory and socialist practice*.[16] This book achieved a certain cult status. It was described by one reviewer some 10 years after publication as of "historical interest" and a "proper subject for analysis and comment," although that reviewer thought it was "superficial and inadequate." The reviewer said the thesis had the obvious advantage of allowing the Marxist Probation Officers "to have their cake and eat it." It meant these officers had the luxury of being in and against the state at the same time, i.e. allowing them to be in paid employment while secretly working to subvert the economic structure which supports them.[17] The main thesis of Walker and Beaumont was that the solution to the problem of crime (and the Probation Officer) was to be found in the Marxian critique, which meant identifying the contradictions of capitalism, and replacing them with a Marxist revolutionary society. Their narrative was based on the premise that crime is a protest against inequalities. That being so the offender becomes the victim and is accorded victim status. That leaves the more traditional victim in a rather difficult position, but it also makes the work of the Probation officer equally difficult, having to decide whose side he/she is on. Whatever the merits or demits of such a critique no government is likely to ignore it, nor likely to forget it.

Being "a social worker of the court"' did not help set out the aims and objectives of the service. Compare this with the Police or Prison Service. Both were able to state their specific aims and objectives, which in both cases were within the compass of what the government saw as working within criminal justice. They saw their aims as protecting the public, whether by "working together to reduce crime," or to protect them by means of secure detention. In contrast the Probation Service lacked an active or pronounced presence. Making things worse, it invariably operated from local (often dingy) offices within which a group of individual officers practised their professional skills, mostly according to their own moral position. Outsiders would have had little understanding about what Probation Officers did, how they went about their task, and what effect they had on the world outside. That the Probation Service was able to muster up support with its petition against privatisation (14th January 2014, with over 35,000 signatures) was a massive achievement given its comparative isolation.

Privatisation put the Probation Service at the centre of the political process. Michael Day writing on "The politics of probation"[18] recognises that probation has always been tied to a political process, not least because governments frame the penal code and decide how much money should be spent on the criminal justice system, and more specifically how much money should be allocated between measures of control and rehabilitation.[19] But privatisation was different. Privatisation involved a mixture of macro and micro politics where demands were made for changes to be made at a national level, and at the minutiae of the local office. In short it included everything that was included within the Probation Service with nowhere left to hide.

Policies and leadership

So much for the structure, what of the policy decisions of the time? Being vulnerable was only part of the explanation as to why the Probation Service was selected for and succumbed to privatisation. A failure to build strategic alliances, and a failure of collective leadership were just as important. In the first the failure was more about remaining isolated within the criminal justice system, and in the second about a failure to understand the government's agenda. Often they merge into a series of lost opportunities as where the Probation Service failed to grasp the significance of certain events, and failed to take advantage of them. NAPO played a part here, not always understanding the significance of new developments.

As a failure to build strategic alliances there was no more glaring example than its failure to incorporate concern for the victims of crime. This is where the service failed to take the initiative: had it done so it could have taken control of a large new area of work, including restorative justice. And the Probation Service was ideally suited to take over the work with victims. It often spoke of its social work roots and aspirations, and here was an opportunity to demonstrate its commitment. However, when it was required to work more closely with victims many Probation Officers resisted the move.[20] The point is well made by the Office for Victims, which said historically probation and parole practices have been offender directed and have ignored or passively responded to the concerns of victims. It said "While offender supervision strategies are aimed at protecting the public as a whole from further victimisation the individual victims are lost."[21]

The Office for Victims point to two particular areas of work which probation services could offer. First, the service has access to both general and specific areas of data that could address victims' needs for information. As a result victims might profit from an understanding about how the Probation Service works. For example, knowing an offender's custody status and understanding that offenders will be held accountable for their actions, either through payments of restitution, or other supervisory conditions, may help the victim reconstitute his/her life after the offence has taken place. Second, victim–offender programmes such as mediation may help victim and offender realise things about each other that can change perspectives and assumptions, i.e. change the offender's perception that no harm was caused by the offence, and the victim's perspective that all offenders are irresponsible and/or dangerous. There are other areas such as offering a therapeutic service. Here the victim may require assistance to overcome a sense of fear that often results in the aftermath of a crime.

The position of the victim within the criminal justice system has changed since the mid-1990s, when there were debates about the victim's role within the trial, or as having an input on the sentence. Prior to that the vacuum had been filled by organisations such as Victim Support, a voluntary organisation, short on resources and accordingly limited in the service it could provide. This was the moment at which the Probation Service should have taken up its position and offered its services. It failed because it was suspicious that the introduction of other professionals would lead to a diminution of the Probation Officers' professional role. Sadly, this is but another occasion where a fear of collaboration held back the service and reduced its impact.

Yet the trend toward recognising the plight of victims, and providing a measure of support, happened to coincide with an interest by government in bringing the victim into a more central position in the criminal justice system. Around 1994 new National Standards included victim issues. Reports to the courts were required to consider the impact of the crime on the victim, a departure from the usual information provided by the social enquiry report. In 2000 under Section 69 (2(a)) the local probation trusts were required to take all reasonable steps to ascertain whether any person should make representation about imposing conditions on certain serious offenders on their release from prison. This was a legal requirement placing on the Probation Service a measure of responsibility for victims. The opportunities were there, all that was needed was the Probation Service to take advantage of them. The result, according to Williams and Goodman[22] was that "inconsistency has bedevilled the Probation Service's work (with victims) from the beginning," albeit that "restorative justice offers a range of challenges."[23]

Victim-centredness, to use a modern term, appears to have posed problems for the Probation Service in that it was said to have produced a conflict of interest. This is described by Nellis and Chui, who say concentrating on the victim creates a climate in which, inadvertently, the harm done to victims, and the shame and scorn which is attached to "perpetrators," make it ever more difficult to acknowledge the needs, rights, and interests of offenders. Apparently it makes it difficult to reintegrate offenders into mainstream society.[24] Whether so or not, this does not seem sufficient for the Probation Service to have ignored the victim. No one is suggesting things would be easy; difficult decisions need to be made about complex issues. For example, Rob Canton and Jane Dominey ask who should represent the victim? Should it be the same officer as the offender's supervisor, and if so might there be a conflict of interest here?[25] Or might affirmation of the rights of victims translate into a wish to induce more punishment on the offender?[26] Nonetheless, one would have expected that their professional skills would be sufficient to handle any conflict that may occur. After all, contradictions and anomalies beset other areas of criminal justice, this is simply another, and should have been dealt with accordingly. Had the Probation Service taken up with victims the door would have been opened to another more lasting initiative, that of restorative justice.

In 2003 the Home Office launched a consultation document on the possibility of introducing restorative justice into its programmes. Restorative justice is a victim focussed resolution that holds offenders to account. Supporters claim it helps offenders take responsibility and make amends for the damage they have done, providing them with an opportunity to learn from their actions and reintegrate into society. Supporters also claim that it empower victims and communities by giving them a chance to communicate with offenders to explain the impact of their crime. The Offender Rehabilitation Act 2014 allows restorative justice to be one of the interventions in Rehabilitation Activity Requirements. It was immensely popular, having a large following, with criminologists, practitioners, and policy makers alike seeing it as having enormous potential. Yet it never really became the central force it was hoped to become, whether in the Probation Service or elsewhere. Some say this was because restorative justice appeared at a time when the Probation Service was beset by other concerns, privatisation being the foremost; others say it was due to poor management; and yet others that it was another example of the service's failure to take on new ideas.

Incidentally, the position after privatisation is that the use of restorative justice has decreased. The NPS is responsible for high risk offenders and restorative justice is not always suitable for that group. Moreover, the CRCs have shown little interest in promoting it. Restorative justice requires a long term commitment for offenders and practitioners alike, and does not produce immediate financial returns for the CRCs. It can be delivered in a variety of ways, sometimes as a post sentence community penalty, sometimes during the prison sentence, and sometimes after release. It has proven popular in some areas, less so in others, due also it seems to poor take up by sentencers, and low recommendations by report writers. As a result, take up is patchy, in some areas such as Manchester there has been a reduction in facilities in 2017 from 96 down to 17.

Yet were it possible to start again and produce a blueprint for a modern Probation Service it would be difficult to leave out the plight of victims. Other European countries such as the Czech Republic and Austria try to be more sensitive to the needs of victims, and include the Probation Service in their vision of a modern criminal justice system, and the Probation Service in Britain should have done more to approximate to that.

The failure of collective leadership is more wide ranging. It shows itself most clearly in the Probation Service's opposition to government, where it believed it knew how to deliver a good service but failed to understand the government's agenda. Take for example the government's intention to introduce "unpaid work." The ACOP response was to post immediate opposition, saying unpaid work stigmatised offenders, and in so doing missing the point that government had a policy to make offenders more publicly accountable. By failing to understand the government's agenda it appeared as if in opposition. Similarly, at an ACOP conference addressed by Michael Howard, he remarked how the Probation Service appeared to be against every suggested proposal.

Consider the introduction of Electronic Monitoring (EM). This shows how the Probation Service failed to accept new technology and ended being marginalised (again), as well as appearing to be truculent and unable to change. It also provides an example of how the division between NAPO and ACOP illustrates the point about a lack of collective leadership. EM, or "tagging" as it has become known, was once opposed by NAPO and others within the service. Their objections were many, some were given in the previous chapter, others argued that "tagging" violated the offenders' human rights, specifically under Articles 3 and 8 of the European Convention on Human Rights; that is those which concerned "inhuman and degrading punishments" and "the right to family life." In fact, there have been no successful challenges to "tagging" on the grounds of human rights.[27] The use of EM has grown and developed since those early days, especially with the introduction of Global Positioning Systems (GPS), which has allowed a much closer watch on high risk and persistent offenders. The expectation is that in future the police and the Probation Service will be able to impose rapid sanctions on those who breach court orders.

ACOP's position was more conciliatory, perhaps recognising or bowing to the inevitable that "tagging" was a new form of control and here to stay. In fact, little research has been conducted on its effectiveness, but it seems likely that many offenders who are "tagged" might otherwise have gone to prison. As Mike Nellis said, they may not like being "tagged" but they like prison less.[28] "Tagging," however, was more than about "pure punishment," as NAPO called it, tagging was also about the introduction of the private sector into the probation world. Again, the hostility by NAPO to new ideas, and its inability to see the merits of a system which was an alternative to prison, albeit more punitive than hitherto, did little to enhance the Probation Service in the eyes of government. It was never considered that an integrated programme could be produced where "tagging" and probation could work together. The result was another example of a service reluctant to embrace change, or at least its representatives were. It was a further example where the Probation Service lost the battle of "care" over "control," where delivering punishment in the community is now accepted practice.

The objection to "tagging" set out the dividing lines between neo liberalism on one side, and traditional ways of working on the other. It also illustrated how the government was losing patience with the Probation Service. So much so that in 1998 a Home Office publication suggested changing its name to the "Public Protection Service" or "Community Justice Enforcement Agency."[29] Those changes were never made but government intentions were clear. But at least the Probation Service did not end up with the same ignominy, as when parole was introduced. Then the service stated quite clearly that it would not undertake the supervision, which it said (again) was punitive and authoritarian. The Home Secretary said in which case he would recruit and train another service to operate parole. The prospects of a rival service, not dissimilar to the American system where probation is separate from parole, was too much. The Probation Service gave in, and parolees were supervised accordingly. It was a classic example of appearing to take up a principled position, but lacking the wherewithal to sustain it.

Finally, as part of the failure of collective leadership consider the service's failure to understand the increasing demand by governments for a more effective service able to cut costs and reduce the prison population. The criticism by Rod Morgan was that offenders being supervised by the Probation Service "are clearly less serious in type."[30] He said that more and more offenders were getting mired deeper and deeper into the criminal justice system for doing less; almost half of all offenders doing community service had no previous convictions, the result being what he called a "silting up" of probation caseloads.[31] The courts were of course ultimately responsible, for it was they who passed the sentence, but "the probation service has played its part" through the recommendation in its court reports. "A declining proportion of the proposals made in Court reports are for fines and discharges."[32] Not only did this produce a greater element of "net widening" but it gave the impression that the service was less interested in being able to work with governments and more concerned with its own preoccupations.

No government is prepared to pay for a social work service applied to low risk offenders with low reoffending rates, while others more serious go unattended. This and other failures by the Probation Service amounts to a systemic lack of understanding of the changes afoot. It suggests too the service did not engage with government or the public, and did not provide a service the government wanted to fund. A less blameworthy approach, and an alternative view, is provided by Loraine Gelsthorpe and Rod Morgan who suggest that the Probation Service was "scapegoated," that is to say it was blamed for failings in the criminal justice system, especially in the 1990s, when other things were going wrong.[33] They argue that during the 1990s and the first years of the new millennium the service was made the scapegoat for a penal system unsustainably overburdened by an increasing number of offenders, and subject to ever intensive punitive sanctions.[34] They say it was dominated by an increase in the rates of criminality, followed by an increase in the use of imprisonment. With longer sentences, this inevitably led to a demand for more punishment. And with higher crime rates came higher rates of imprisonment. These were some of the inadequacies, say Gelsthorpe and Morgan, which led to "scapegoating," the main features being what they call sentencing drift. This means the Probation Service found itself with larger caseloads but greater proportions of minor offenders with less serious offending histories, and an unjoined nature of the Probation and Prison Service, i.e. prison and probation were not working together.

Unfortunately Gelsthorpe and Morgan give no evidence that the Probation Service was "scapegoated" and selected out for opprobrium any more than other aspect of criminal justice. Inevitably, the Probation Service would be asked to make its contribution to government aims at crime reduction, and this, it seems, it failed to do. To make matters worse in 2006 there were two reports on events leading up to the separate murders of offenders subject to probation supervision. The first report identified "serious probation failings" in the nature of that supervision, which involved two murders, and the second report, which involved the murder of one person also subject to probation supervision, also identified other "serious failings." Unsurprisingly, the Probation Service was subject to intense criticism, but in this respect Gelsthorpe and Morgan are correct as the service became incorrectly linked to other failings within the Home Office. This was the time when there was a crisis over immigration, and taken together this led John Reid the Home Secretary in 2006 to say that the Home Office "was not fit for purpose."

The NOMS merger

The Probation Service was also the unfortunate recipient of the NOMS merger – again, a point made in the previous chapter. Not only did the Prison Service in NOMS overwhelm the Probation Service by its sheer size, but the Probation Service found itself within an organisation that was frequently criticised for its poor management and failure to provide effective financial monitoring. For example, in its assessment of one project aimed at implementing a single offender management IT system, NOMS was criticised as having "Contractual arrangements with its key suppliers (which) were weak and its supplier management poor."[35] Or again, this also from the same Audit Office Report:

> The initiative to introduce a single management database has been expensive and ultimately unsuccessful. These problems could have been avoided if NOMS had established realistic budgets, timescales and governance for the project at the start and followed basic

project management principles in its implementation. In delivering the now reduced programme NOMS needs to focus on better financial controls and more effective management oversight."[36]

The Probation Service was unfortunate therefore to have been overwhelmed, first by the prison service to create NOMS, but then to be tarnished by association with an agency offering such a poor style of management. It was bad luck, if luck can ever be part of policy, and if so, then bad luck also to have a dedicated Minister at the Ministry of Justice during the Coalition period who was so eager to introduce privatisation. But perhaps one makes one's own luck, in which case the Probation Service should not complain about the outcome.

Accommodating to change

No one finds it easy to accommodate or adjust to change, but the Probation Service seems to have found it harder than most. When the demands of government were sounding loud and clear the service remained locked into a belief system that meant it was seemingly unmoved by the turmoil surrounding it. One can see this as its strength as being inviolable, or perhaps see it as a weakness as being unable to adjust to change, depending of course on one's point of view. The outcome has been a divided service, and a loss of prestige and status. This must have its consequential impact on other parts of the criminal justice system including offenders and victims who are affected by these changes.

It is not clear if there was anything the Probation Service could have done to ameliorate its position. It is doubtful if more intense opposition would have had much of an impact, or that greater cooperation would have changed the government's mind. Successive governments seem to have been fixed on privatisation as an end product, and certain that their neo liberal strategy was the correct course of action. Nonetheless, the service might have had some influence about a number of the details proposed; for example it might have changed the government's thinking on working with victims, or on unpaid work, or even on EM, or insisted that government required more careful planning and piloting before decisions were made, especially about *Transforming Rehabilitation* and about a greater measure of flexibility between the NPS and the

CRCs. Most of all it could have had an impact early on other matters were it to have been more flexible and shifted its stance from its implacable position on being "social workers of the courts" to "Probation Officers of the courts." Who knows what such changes might have brought about? The results? They are difficult to assess, but they might have meant seizing opportunities that were otherwise missed, avoiding events otherwise misunderstood, and not being part of heedless and unnecessary opposition brought about by failing to understand the spirit of the times.

In the next two chapters I want to look more closely at what privatisation means. I want to see how it works in practice before finally speculating about the possible future of the service.

Notes

1 Mair G (2016) "A difficult trip I think": the end days of the probation service in England and Wales? *European Journal of Probation*. Vol. 8, No. 1, pp. 3–15. Pg. 3.
2 Ibid. p. 6.
3 Carter P (2003) *Managing offenders reducing crime: the correctional services review*. The Strategic Unit. P. 34.
4 Lol Burke. Pers. Com.
5 NAPO evidence to the Justice Committee's Report on the Government's Transforming Rehabilitation Programme. Para 16–20.
6 Day M (1987) The politics of probation. In Harding J (ed) *Probation and the Community*. Tavistock, pp. 21–34. P. 32.
7 Ibid. P. 30.
8 Ibid. P. 33.
9 Budd J and Knivett T. Pers. Com.
10 NAPO (2011) Briefing paper. Privatisation and the Probation Service.
11 Ibid. P. 9.
12 Mair G and Burke L (2012) *Redemption, rehabilitation and risk management*. Routledge. P. 86.
13 Quoted in Chui W and Nellis M (2003) Creating the National Probation Service. New wine in old bottles. In Chui W and Nellis M (eds) *Moving probation forward*. Pearson Longman, pp. 1–19. Pg. 14.
14 Budd J and Knivett T. Pers. Com.
15 Budd J and Knivett T. Pers. Com.
16 The book by Walker H and Beaumont W (1981) was entitled *Probation work: critical theory and socialist practice* and published by Blackwell
17 The reviewer was Robert Harris in a review entitled "Poor Marx." *Probation Journal*, Vol. 38, No. 3, pp 144–145. Pg. 144.

18 Day M (1987) op. cit. Pg. 21–34.
19 Ibid. P. 21.
20 Williams B and Goodman H (2007) Working for and with victims of crime. In Gelsthorpe L and Morgan R (eds) *Handbook of probation*. Willan Publishing. pp. 518–541. Pg. 521.
21 Office for Victims (1999) *Promising victim-related practitioners and strategies in probation and parole*. US Department of Justice. Pg. 1.
22 Williams B and Goodman H (2007) op. cit. Pg. 536.
23 Ibid. Pg. 536.
24 Nellis M and Chui W (2003) The end of Probation? In Nellis M and Chui W (eds) *Moving probation forward*. Pearson Longman. pp. 261–275. Pg. 269.
25 See particularly Nellis M (2003) Electronic Monitoring and the future of probation. In Chui W.H. and Nellis M. (eds) *Moving probation forward*. Pearson Longman, pp. 245–260, for a discussion on "tagging" and the Probation Service. Pg. 244.
26 Ibid. Pg. 242.
27 See Lockart-Miriams G, Pickles C, and Crowhurst E (2015) for a discussion on later developments of EM. Lockart-Miriams G, Pickles C, and Crowhurst E (2015) *Cutting crime: the role of tagging in offender management*. Reform Research Trust.
28 Nellis M (2003) op. cit.
29 Home Office. (1998) Joining forces to protect the public: prisons-probation. A consultation document. Stationery Office.
30 Morgan R (2003) Thinking about the demand for probation service. *Probation Journal*. Vol. 50, No. 1, pp 7–19. Pg. 15.
31 Ibid. Pg. 15.
32 Ibid. Pg. 15.
33 Gelsthorpe L and Morgan R (2007) Introduction. In Gelsthorpe L and Morgan R (eds) *Handbook of probation*. Willan Publishing. pp. 1–19.
34 Ibid. Pg. 12.
35 House of Commons National Audit Office. (2009) National Offender Management Information System. The Stationary Office. (June). Pg. 7.
36 Ibid.

4

PRIVATISATION AT WORK

Separate services, opening up the market and Payment by Results

On the 9th January 2013 the Coalition Government published its White Paper *Transforming Rehabilitation: a revolution in the way we manage offenders*. Its intentions were clear; to privatise the Probation Service's core work. Later, in a Consultation Document on May 2013 the government formally announced it would go ahead with the programme. This was followed by the Offender Rehabilitation Act 2014 which put many of the proposals into law. The Act received the Royal Assent on the 13th May 2014, an unusually short time for legislation to be introduced and completed, a point regarded by many in Parliament and elsewhere as of unseemly haste.[1]

The then Justice Minister Chris Grayling in his Foreword to the consultation on *Transforming Rehabilitation* set out details of the problem. He said;

> Last year around 600,000 crimes were committed by those who had broken the law. Nearly half of those released from prison went on to reoffend, in many cases not just once but time and again. Despite increases in spending under previous Governments reoffending rates have barely changed. This can't go on. I want to ensure that all those who break the law are not only punished, but

also receive mentoring and rehabilitative support to get their lives back on track so they do not commit crime again.[2]

Few would disagree. The reoffending rate, or more accurately the reconviction rate, for no one knows how much reoffending occurs, is chronically high and has been so for a number of years. This group, those sentenced to short terms of imprisonment, have that very high reconviction rate. Grayling decided to tackle this, and was correct to do so. He was also correct to say that if successful it will be a massive achievement. Given the chronicity and size of the problem he thought we should expect only gradual improvement, at least in the first few years. From that point onward more tangible gains would be expected. He placed the Probation Service at the centre of his proposals because he said rehabilitation lies within the service's traditions.

The usual parliamentary procedure for such a course of action would be as follows; first there would be a Green Paper which would set out the problem and suggest solutions. This would be followed by a White Paper setting out proposals in more detail and inviting discussion. A follow up White Paper would show where amendments were to be made. Piloting in some form would follow, alongside the publication of a set of costings showing the overall costs of the project and any expected savings. The full parliamentary process would then follow.

In this case no such standard procedures applied. There was no Green Paper, although there were two White Papers. There were no pilot projects, at least none in the accepted sense; that is to say two were started in Peterborough and Doncaster prisons but were never completed, and anyway as said earlier they involved only prisoners on voluntary not on mandatory supervision. Again, as said earlier there were no detailed figures on costings; nothing on start up costs, or on expected running costs. Nor were there figures on expected savings, at least none that were made public. Where information has been provided it has been almost casually slipped into the public domain – as where over £200m was paid in 2017 to the private sector but only discovered by *Private Eye* after detailed investigation (see below). These and other shortcomings have been highlighted in Parliament and by numerous commentators.

Before looking at the proposals in more detail I want to make three unrelated points. First, if only to repeat an earlier point, *Transforming*

Rehabilitation did not identify a new problem, but it did offer a new solution in so far as it divided the service into public and private sector organisations. The reconviction rate of short term prisoners, and the proposed solution, which involving linking the Prison and Probation services, has been known for a long time, and the solutions, albeit in slightly different forms, proposed before. For example, in a report by the Social Exclusion Unit in 2002, *Reducing reoffending by ex-prisoners,* the problem was highlighted by Tony Blair in the Foreword. He said much that was similar to that highlighted by Chris Grayling some 12 years later, namely that three in five prisoners are reconvicted within two years of leaving prison. The solution in the earlier report was also very much the same; Blair said he wanted to link the Prison Service to the Probation Service. Offenders released from prison would then find that there would be a range of services available, with various stakeholders working together. Differences, such as there were between Blair and Grayling, centred around the privatisation of sections of the Probation Service. That is to say Grayling sought a form of privatisation which involved the creation of Community Rehabilitation Companies (CRCs) and a system of Payment by Results (PbR) – said to be an innovation in criminal justice. Blair made no such proposals.

Second, there has been much acclaim about the general set of aims, but a barrage of criticisms about the solutions and the way privatisation has been introduced. Mostly, the criticisms have been about a lack of planning and a lack of information about costs. Criticisms have been extensive and unrelenting, with protests taking numerous forms. Aside from the usual methods of protesting, there was on the 5th November 2013 a 24 hour strike by members of NAPO. They protested in a manner unprecedented in the Probation Service's history. The Justice Minister's response was to say strikers were simply in favour of the *status quo*. That, he said, meant giving support to high offending rates, and not providing the necessary rehabilitation for about 50,000 or so short term newly released prisoners who were without supervision and go on to commit further offences. Then there was a Probation Petition (on the 14th January 2014) which had over 35,000 signatories. Petitioners opposed plans to privatise probation, with their objections mainly against neo liberalism and the introduction of the private sector. They wanted those convicted by a criminal court to be supervised by a publicly accountable Probation Service. The government's response to the petition as to the strike, and as to many other criticisms, was simply to ignore them. In fact, Chris Grayling merely repeated what he had said many times before; that he was opening up the market to a diverse range of new rehabilitative providers so that we can get the best out of the public voluntary and private sector at both local and national levels. Unfortunately the Justice Committees in 2014 and 2018 concluded there were few if any discernible results.[3]

Third, the data presented here on the CRCs and the National Probation Service (NPS) such as there is, comes largely from HM Inspectorate of Probation, or from anecdotal evidence gained from the occasional contact with members of staff. CRCs and the National Probation Service have been reluctant to open their doors to scrutiny. This has placed limitations on discussions, particularly about contracts and payments, but also about the day to day activities, including relationships between the two groups, and their links with outside agencies.

On one side of the debate were those supporting the neo liberal position, that is to say, where instead of government funding projects from tax receipts, the private sector would be contracted to complete and manage the projects. On the other were those wishing to retain the system whereby the public sector deals exclusively with public sector matters. It was a rehearsal of earlier arguments involving the Private Finance Initiative (or PFI) which became popular from about 1992 onwards. Privatisation of probation follows a traditional PFI model.[4]

There were five major aims in *Transforming Rehabilitation*. It was claimed they would change the rehabilitation of selected offenders to the point where it would reduce the reconviction rate and alter the way offenders were dealt with. They are:

1. A split in the provision of community services between a National Probation Service (NPS) and private sector companies (CRCs);
2. Opening up the market to a diverse range of providers;
3. A "Payment by Results" incentive to pay for reductions in reoffending;
4. Joined up "Through The Gate" resettlement services across most prisons and the community, and;
5. A new Institute of Probation.

In this Chapter I want to look at the first three, which involve splitting up the Probation Service, in effect producing the National Probation Service alongside the Community Rehabilitation Companies. I also want to look at the way the market has been opened, if at all, and then at Payment by Results. In Chapter 5 I want to look at Through The Gate services (TTG), and at the new Probation Institute.

1. A split in the provision of community services between a National Probation Service (NPS) and private sector companies (CRCs)

First, what of the split in the provision of community services between a NPS and private sector CRCs? This is a key feature of privatisation, the fulcrum on which so much else depends. It is also one of the most controversial, if only because it changed dramatically the nature of the service, as well as eventually bringing between 45,000 and 50,000 offenders into the new system – estimates vary, but for the moment leave this aside. The CRCs did not suddenly become responsible for that large number, only for those convicted after a certain date, but the overall figure would amount to over 45,000. That apart, it was never made clear why there should be such a split, except to hope that practices would improve, as would facilities for the rehabilitation of offenders. These however are hardly sufficient to justify such a radical policy. There was no detailed discussion, or an examination of the implications. It seemed as if the policy was presented as simply based on a series of assertions, namely that privatisation was by definition the best way forward, and PbR the means by which the policy was to be funded. Alternatives were not considered. Nonetheless, Chris Grayling, ever the enthusiast, said, "This competition will deliver real value for the hardworking taxpayer and ensure we get the best in the business when it comes to rehabilitating offenders." He said, "We are doing business differently."[5] What he didn't say was that two companies, one of which was Sodexo, represented more than half the devolved Probation Service.

Yet whilst the government believed that the split between the NPS and CRCs would have the capacity to improve working practices – indeed that was a key aim – numerous commentators suggested it had the capacity to do otherwise, i.e. to create divisions. Nonetheless, the government believed that many first class projects had already been developed by the private sector, especially in the field of substance abuse, and there was every reason to believe others would follow. None of these statements however answered the basic question; which is, was it necessary to split the service in this way? Whenever that question was raised the response was less of a justification, more a description of how best to proceed. So, the government said in its White Paper in 2013 that

> Our strategy for reform includes a strong NPS tasked with protecting the public from the most dangerous offenders; a new mix of providers equipped with the flexibility and the right incentives to reduce reoffending; and some important systemic changes to provided effective rehabilitation to those who need it most...[6]

That White Paper contained numerous aims to reduce offending but all were largely aspirational. For example, it said "this new mix of providers" alongside "important systemic changes" would be effective, but not how or why this should be so. One would have expected detailed justifications, hopefully a discussion on alternatives, or perhaps data from a pilot project on which to base some evidence. For even if we assume there were good reasons for introducing the private sector into a new type of Probation Service, and assume too that we know some of the right incentives to reduce offending (for the moment take no issue with this), other options were available. It would have been possible to introduce projects from the private sector and integrate them gradually into the existing service. Assessments could then have been made to see if integration had been successful. After all, there was no need to rush matters. The problem has existed for decades, and waiting another year or two would make little difference in the overall scheme of things. A step by step approach, with each project evaluated might take longer, but would not produce the levels of uncertainty, or the upheaval promoted by the current changes.

Another alternative, and an oft suggested one, was to simply expand the service. That would mean giving it extra responsibilities and taking on more work with the prisons, including more mandatory supervision of prisoners. That, it was said, would be more effective and keep the service in its current format.

> A simple solution to this would be to extend supervision of these (offenders) to the current probation trusts which have a proven track record in reducing offending rates rather than give this important work to unproven organisations driven by a profit motive.[7]

Changes could be made without producing a resulting upheaval. For in spite of earlier criticisms, the service it seems was well equipped to undertake this task. After being told by John Reid in 2007 "it was not fit for purpose," it was now being praised for its professionalism and quality of work. Shortly before privatisation it won the British Quality Foundation Gold Medal for "excellence in recognition of outstanding continued commitment to excellence over a number of years." The Minister for Prisons and Probation publicly gave his support. He said "This prestigious award recognises the professionalism of probation staff and the excellence of their work."[8] Not only that, but according to the National Offender Management Service (NOMS)[9] in 2011, all probation trusts were rated as either "good" or "exceptional." None required changes. In the circumstances no wonder NAPO thought it was "very odd" to privatise it.

It is easy to see therefore why some critics saw privatisation as unnecessary, or as far as Julian Le Vay was concerned, unnecessary and wrong. Writing mainly of prisons but in this case considering the impact of privatisation on probation, he said it created huge difficulties and risks.[10] He also said it required high levels of competence in contracting and contract management that the Ministry of Justice has recently been shown to lack. He noted too the breakneck speed at which the proposals were implemented, views which coincided with those of NAPO who also called the programme a recipe for disaster; not only disastrous for the Probation Service, but for the public generally. NAPO thought the introduction of the CRCs posed risks and threats to public safety, calling them untried, untested, and ideologically flawed.

Sometimes it appeared as if the government blamed the Probation Service for all the failings, with the service being responsible for having to introduce privatisation. For example, Chris Grayling said that the number of people who go on to commit crime after being released from prison is too high. That may be true, but the answer however did not lie in failings of the Probation Service. The Probation Service does not manage these offenders on release, so it is disingenuous to blame it for such failures. Lord Ramsbotham in the House of Lords Debates on the Second Reading of the Bill also said he was uneasy about such statements by the Justice Secretary, who said that despite significant increases in spending on probation under the previous government, almost half of those released from prison still go on to reoffend within 12 months. Lord Ramsbotham said this confirmed his worst fear, as "this is one group of offenders for whom the Probation Service has no responsibility…"[11]

Others, in a similar vein said the service was beginning to take on the responsibility for this group of offenders anyway, so that what has been happening was not necessary. Or again, this from Rob Allen (2013) who said "progress … would be much more likely by building on the experience of Probation Trusts and their local partners rather than creating yet another new structure."[12]

But would it? Not, it seems, according to certain government sources who said that retaining the existing structure, or rather simply expanding it was too costly. In an open letter Mr. Andrew Selous, Parliamentary Under Secretary of State for Justice (16th March 2015) said it would have been possible for government to retain existing structures, but it wisely chose otherwise. For in order to provide a better form of rehabilitation, and with better value for the taxpayer "we could only do this by bringing the best of the public, voluntary and private sector to work with offenders in order to reduce their offending rates."[13] That may be so, but again a less radical proposal ought also to have been considered. Incidentally, there was no recovery plan were things to go wrong, and as far as I can see little enthusiasm generally for the privatisation of the service outside a small circle of enthusiasts.

A net result is of a privatisation programme, the outcome of which involved considerable structural changes which has divided the service into public and private sections. Both organisations employ Probation Officers but they do different work, and operate from different locations. It is a structure unique to modern criminal justice, whether in

Britain or elsewhere. It was based on a belief, and a hope, that the private sector would work alongside its public counterparts, and that working together would produce results which have hitherto defied earlier attempts at a solution. The question therefore is can this privatisation programme succeed where others have failed? The answer it seems, according to Chris Grayling, is that we must wait and see; he believes there are many problems to be resolved, and a considerable distance to travel before the programme can be adjudged, successful or otherwise, but he believes success will come. Many of the inspection reports are less sanguine, some being slightly optimistic, but most others offering little or no hope for the future.

If this new system is to move forward, then hopefully it will take place in a more measured setting. What are the likely effects on the probation staff working the new system, let alone on the respective service users? After all, we now have two probation systems, separated by a clear ideological divide, each dealing with different subsets of offenders.

An obvious problem was that dividing the service might produce tensions and competition between the two groups. For although all working in the NPS and CRCs are classified as Probation Officers (or Probation Services Officers for the lower grades), they now work for different employers. Nor did they necessarily choose to which organisation they should belong. Their allocation was decided initially according to their existing caseloads, where those with the highest risk offenders went to the NPS, others to CRCs. Allocation was based on assessments by a local Risk Assessment Unit. Offenders allocated to NPS remain with NPS. Staff were allocated on a randomly chosen date in the latter part of 2013. Apparently almost all of the Probation Officers allocated to the NPS said they agreed with the assessment compared with only about one half of those allocated to the CRCs. So much so, that in the first few months of privatisation NAPO reports that over 500 officers appealed against their assignment to CRCs, with over 100 being successful. Moreover, a large number of staff allocated to the CRCs were declared redundant or left the service with severance pay – about 40% according to some estimates.

The legislation therefore produced two separate organisations with different aims and working practices. From the outset predictions were made that divisions of this sort would be difficult to sustain. It was said they would create tensions which would lead to different forms of practice, all to the detriment to the service generally. One could see how these could occur. The NPS is a government body which oversees high risk offenders as they are reintegrated into the community. It has additional duties such as preparing presentence reports for the courts, preparing prisoners for release, and *liaising* with victims of sexual assault, or violent encounters where the offender is in a mental health facility, or has been incarcerated for longer than one year. In contrast, the CRCs are private bodies concerned with delivering a resettlement service for all other offenders, including those released from custody. They manage low and medium risk offenders in the community, and are designed to deliver a different range of services, including the government's payback scheme for those on unpaid work requirements. They are also managers of senior attendance centres.

When assessing the impact of privatisation, which for these purposes means the division of the service into public and private sectors, it is of course easy to emphasise differences and draw attention to potential conflicts between members of the different organisations. Similarly, it is easy to ignore the countless agreements in working practices that take place daily between members as they work alongside each other. I do not want to overstate any signs of conflict, and I want to recognise that cooperation between the NPS and CRCs is likely to be more the order of the day. But splitting the service in this way provides the potential for disagreements, many of which have implications for working practices now and later. Inevitably, differences will appear, whether they be in attitude or approach. It is not apparent at this early stage what is likely to happen, but already there are hints that areas of conflict exist, with others likely in the near future. I have listed what I think are three major areas of conflict surrounding the privatisation programme; the status of the groups, their different conditions of service, and the required communication between the two parties.

First the status divisions. Quite soon after the service was divided there began to appear differences in perceived status. Those officers allocated to the NPS began to be seen as more important (they were dealing with the higher risk offenders), and therefore of a higher status than those in the CRCs. John Deering and Martina Feilzer, in their research on the likely workings of privatisation, albeit three months before it formally began, found that a number of officers saw the NPS as "some kind of elite" with a "them and us" mentality already producing "an elitist NPS and a second rate CRC."[14] The situation is likely to be exacerbated as NPS will continue to employ trained probation staff, but the CRCs will employ a range of staff, not all with appropriate levels of training and competence.[15] The less qualified, the Probation Services Officers, have tended to remain with the CRCs. Nor was there any obligation on the CRCs to be responsible for training. This may be a cost saving measure for them, and an expensive one for the state, but to be responsible for training is to control the inputs to the service, whether they be in terms of the staff selected, or the type of work undertaken. As Deering and Feilzer say, differences in training and qualifications are only likely to widen over time, eventually making a two tier system inevitable, with a clear hierarchy and sense of importance. As one officer told Deering and Feilzer; initially staff will be immediate colleagues – often they share the same premises – but this will gradually change as knowledge is lost and opportunities are reduced.[16] Splitting the service in this way therefore had serious dangers. It seems most staff with the full time Probation Officer qualifications prefer to work with the NPS, despite the fact that similar skills are required on both sides of the programme.

Second, conditions of service. Although required to work together, NPS and the CRC employees have increasingly different priorities. They also have different geographical areas of work. In Nottingham for example, the NPS have offices in the Magistrates Courts building, the CRCs are located in various parts of the city. This is an obvious example of different levels of importance. But of course there is no need for the CRCs to have an office in the courts, they are not involved in court based work, and have no role in the courts. Court work is undertaken by the NPS. This means CRC Probation Officers are cut off from traditional probation practice, and from their traditional power base. Over time they will have less and less experience and understanding of the courts and, equally important, the courts will have less and less understanding of them.

Moreover, their career patterns and prospects are different; for example those working for the CRCs are promoted using different criteria from those in the NPS. Security of employment also differs.

Those in the NPS retain their public sector security whilst those in the CRCs will be aware that contracts may fail. As staff costs are the largest costs, reductions in staff, or increases in caseloads are another possible outcome, and again this has already occurred with large numbers of redundancies reported by some CRCs (see Chapter 6). The likelihood is that a different world view will emerge, and one suspects it has already done so. Those working in the CRCs say they are more cost conscious than before, recognising that payments are made according to strict requirements involving assessments, reporting, etc. Working in the CRCs means being more aware of costs, or as one CRC officer said, not doing so means no one gets paid. The commissioner/provider model forces the CRCs to work according to specified outputs defined as measurable and achievable. No such demands are placed on the NPS.

Assessments of offenders are also likely to be affected. Assessments are more than identifying what is wrong, they are about suggesting the means to put things right. "Good assessments are about exploration," meaning that assessments are also about resources. That of course raises other questions; whether such resources are to be available to the CRCs in equal amount and quality as for the NPS? If not, will assessments differ? (An example of the impact of cost reduction can be seen in modern psychiatric reports to the court, where once a report would say "the offender has a mental disorder and treatment is offered," now they simply say "the offender has a mental disorder." And these reports do not affect CRCs.) The Annual Report by HM Inspectors of Probation in 2017 confirmed what is suspected, that there exists "a two tier and fragmented service with individuals being supervised by the NPS more effectively overall." The Inspectorate goes on to point out somewhat tellingly that "Of course the NPS is funded differently and more generously."[17]

The third likely area of conflict concerns the levels of communications between the groups. It is difficult to avoid the obvious conclusion that having two groups, with different employers and with different aims and objectives, require a high level of agreement and cooperation. Probation work, after all, involves a complicated arrangement whereby the NPS manages the high risk cases, and also deals with the courts and breach proceedings. In contrast the CRCs deal with medium and low risk cases but require agreement from the NPS to breach an offender under their supervision. Some offenders may change their risk category, moving from a low risk to a higher risk or vice versa. Because of the decision to keep high risk offenders with the NPS the government has had to design a system for transferring cases from the private to the State sector should risks escalate. The Probation Service in December 2015 was supervising 220,000 offenders, of whom 25% change risk during the course of their order or licence. The situation is further complicated as that each year about 400 serious offences are committed by offenders on licence, mainly when the offender is going through a period of change, including a change of supervising officer. These serious offences include murder, manslaughter, robbery, and rape. If there are insufficient staff in the private sector with the ability to recognise the necessary levels of risk it is likely that such incidents will increase.

To operate effectively information must flow freely across boundaries. The evidence thus far suggests tensions and suspicions exist between the two groups which can only have a deleterious effect on the service, and on the offenders who are to report and be supervised. Communication was always going to be an issue, whether between individuals or groups. Unfortunately, and within a very short time – in some cases even before the formal break occurred – problems appeared. It had always been recognised that good communications were necessary, not just for the benefit of the officers, but for public safety generally. The danger was always that short term self-interests might emerge.[18] Sadly, it seems some of those early fears were justified. Within a short time it was reported that some basic grade officers in some areas stopped talking to others in the opposite organisation. Friction at a basic organisational level began to appear. For example, the National Audit Office (in 2016) noticed that many junior staff at the CRCs considered their NPS contacts to be unduly dismissive and critical, whilst their NPS counterparts thought CRC contacts were not providing them with the necessary information because they had become too focussed on commercial interests.[19]

A briefing by NAPO on the 9th January 2015[20] talks of "significant concerns regarding the stability of the service and service delivery". It lists a number of areas, one of which is of staff shortages leading to high workloads and high sickness levels. Apparently, within a short time of privatisation agency staff were being recruited to the CRCs with all the attendant problems of confidentiality that such staff introduce. The result is that the Ministry of Justice has, according to NAPO, acknowledged the problem, and accepted that there are significant concerns regarding the stability of the service and service delivery. NAPO wanted contracts withheld until the service was in what it called a steady state. It said something similar before privatisation, and continued the same theme afterwards. Given the way the whole programme has being implemented, and at such speed, there was never any chance of that.

Deering and Feilzer make the important point that questions of communication have soon became overlaid by issues of trust.[21] They say where trust is absent, confidentiality is dangerously close to being absent also. The implications are important. Offenders may remain unsupervised, unsupported, and easily lost in the system to the detriment to all concerned, including the public and the organisation responsible for their supervision. Julian Le Vay[22] notes that the criminal justice system is not historically known for the fluency of information flow across boundaries. That being so it seems the system produced here is almost set up to fail, or put in a slightly different way and to use modern jargon is "operationally challenging."

It is not just about communication at the human level which is problematic, but at the technical level also. I want to say more about the poor quality of IT systems within the Probation Service in the last chapter, here I only want to highlight various reports by HM Inspectorate of probation which have repeatedly drawn attention to this matter. These reports constantly state that the poor quality of IT systems has been a major contributing factor to what is seen as a systemic failure to communicate between the two groups. The poor quality of IT systems in the Probation Service has been widely known; they pre date privatisation, but privatisation has brought these deficiencies to the fore. Privatisation has simply made worse any existing deficiency by dividing the service into separate groups.

It may be too early to assess the full impact of this aspect of privatisation. What is clear however is that it is no longer possible to compare the two systems, we are simply not comparing like with like. Differences between NPS and the CRCs are now sufficiently clear as to talk of two different Probation Services. And the longer the division continues the wider will be the gap, leading quite soon to what Deering and Feilzer regard as a "chasm."[23] It is strange that there was little or no public discussion on the likely impact on the respective groups of differing organisational demands, or of differing employment contracts. The expectations seem to have been that the two groups will immediately work in harmony and work together for the greater good. That they may do so eventually is to be hoped, but in the meantime it seems attention needs to be given to some basic matters such as easing communications and finding ways to allay fears amongst those in the CRCs that they are not second class Probation Officers.

2. Opening up the market to a diverse range of providers

Returning to those five aims listed above, the second was to open up the market to a diverse range of providers. This means granting contracts to the private companies who were the successful bidders, and for the companies to extend their range of activities. CRCs have been recruited from three major sources: the private sector, the voluntary sector, and charities. These, for example, are the successful CRCs in different areas of England:

Bedfordshire, Northants, Cambridgeshire and Hertfordshire. The CRCs were Sodexo in partnership with NACRO.

Derbyshire, Leicestershire Nottinghamshire and Rutland. The CRC was with The Redwing Reoffending Partnership.

London. The CRC was MTC Novo in partnership with 6 other companies. MTC Novo is in joint partnership with RISE a probation staff community interest company, Band of Brothers a Charity, Manchester College a public sector provider, Sanctuary Supported Living a social landlord, Thames Valley Partnership a Charity and Amey a private Company.

The new contracts involve 3 Levels of potential providers. Level 1, the top level is for the owners of the CRCs who are the lead providers. Levels 2 and 3 are for the others who are more akin to subcontractors. Each CRC will be expected to develop its own supply chain consisting of these subcontractors. The difference between those listed in Levels 2 and 3 is such that Level 2 is likely to be for larger voluntary sector organisations, and Level 3 for the smaller ones. It is not altogether clear what this means in practice, nor does it seem particularly relevant. It is a complicated structure, difficult to understand and probably difficult to manage.

Incidentally, as part of the bidding process bidders were asked to suggest ways of reducing costs. Those most often identified were about replacing inefficient technologies, implementing mobile working practices for reporting, and introducing more group work, the latter called the "cohort model" of working. They also identified other inefficiencies within the public sector, none of which were contentious. Others however were, especially those involving what was called "implementing mobile working practices." This was a coded way of saying they planned to introduce electronic kiosks for offenders reporting to their Probation Officers – a suggestion which later brought forth some highly critical comments from the Probation Inspectorate.

Changes began in June 2013. The first hint of what was to come was from a leaked risk register compiled by the Ministry of Justice. It said contracts for the new rehabilitation companies would be awarded by the beginning of October 2014. These contracts would, it was said, open up the market to a diverse range of new rehabilitative providers, aimed at getting the best out of the public, voluntary, and private sectors at both local and national level. On the 31st March 2014 the government announced that existing probation trusts would be replaced by a National Probation Service dealing with the highest risk offenders. The majority of other offenders would be transferred to the newly created Community Rehabilitation Companies, which were to be companies formed by the Ministry of Justice. Initially they were listed as companies limited by shares and owned by the government (the Ministry of Justice), where they were to remain until final contracts were awarded in December 2014. Eventually, 21 Community Rehabilitation Companies were created from the 35 original probation trusts. Staff were allocated either side of the divide.

Thirty bidders passed the first stage to win the 21 contracts – 20 for regions throughout England, and 1 for Wales. The main bids came from 30 organisations; 11 later withdrew leaving 19, but not all made bids. The final result was 8 successful companies for the 21 CRCs. (They were Sodexo, Working Links, ARCC, Purple Futures, MTCnovo, Reducing Reoffending, People Plus, and Seetec.) Serco and G4S withdrew from the competition after irregularities in their earlier contracts with electronic monitoring, these companies incidentally having the most experience of the criminal justice system. All the successful companies were said to have some degree of experience working with offenders, or with access to some aspects of the criminal justice system, but it was not clear what that meant, or how much experience that entailed. Looking through the list it is doubtful if some had anything more than a passing connection

The bidding process was aimed at providing competition to deliver probation services. It did not begin well. To assist the bidders there was a data room with data provided in electronic form, but unfortunately some of it was out of date − staffing figures for example − and other data was difficult to obtain from the equipment provided. When the final contracts were awarded they were almost impenetrable in their legalise. Nonetheless, the big bidders had to show that they were engaging the voluntary sector in a way that was more than tokenism. The fear was that the big bidders would use the voluntary sector as "bid candy," i.e, mention the smaller agencies regularly in the bids but ignore them later. The government's intention was that the voluntary sector would also bid for contracts alongside others in the private sector, but this also did not turn out as expected. The voluntary sector simply could not provide the financial guarantees that were available to the larger bidders in the private sector. Moreover the contracts themselves were said to be so complicated that only the large companies had the expertise to understand them, and the cost of professional and legal fees necessary was such that only the large companies could afford to negotiate them. The net result was a less than satisfactory outcome for the smaller companies.

The other problem was the responsibility imposed on the CRCs for delivering a rehabilitation service to offenders. Rehabilitation has always been central to the work of the Probation Service and the CRCs were simply required to follow that tradition. It is not clear however if they are doing so, or rather if they were, then they might be following a more weakened version. The more formal and inclusive definition of rehabilitation involves a process and an outcome, the former means helping the individual offender to desist from crime, and the outcome involves the restoration of the individual to the rights and obligations of full citizenship.[24] The offence is the justification for the state to intervene in the offender's life. Rehabilitation as used in *Transforming Rehabilitation* is more of a prescriptive term, non-specific, without demanding that the CRCs define what is meant by it, or set out the duties and practices involved. It simply includes supervising low and medium risk offenders and providing a range of rehabilitation activities to all offenders including those supervised by the NPS through a new system of payment incentives. CRCs are also required to refer offenders who become high risk to the NPS.

The introduction of the CRCs represent a sea change in the history of probation and a departure from all the earlier traditions of the service. A private sector Probation Service would have been unthinkable to those working a generation ago, yet here was the private sector required to pursue a policy of rehabilitation, however loosely defined, and in circumstances which were encouraged by government. Unsurprisingly, the many critics of privatisation doubt the possibility of the private sector being able to deliver such a programme. Lol Burke and Steve Collett, for example, see little hope of the CRCs being able to pursue rehabilitation and so improve the offender's conditions. They believe rehabilitation is best served by a local agency fully integrated and publicly accountable. They also believe that desistance takes time and is not amenable to simple binary measures as required for payments to the private sector as with Payment by Results (see below). Moreover, they say, the introduction of the private sector into a criminal justice forum undermines a sense of public responsibility. Essentially their argument is that the market concept is alien to traditions of public service.[25] They go further and argue that privatisation is part of the process, of what they call punitive bifurcation whereby criminal justice policy and practice is a way of separating the less serious offenders from the more dangerous in order to impose more punitive and restrictive sentences.[26]

A similar point is made by Rob Canton and Jane Dominey[27] who argue that probation is more than a set of services to bring about selected ends. If it were so then the provider of those services becomes unimportant. They suggest that probation, which for these purposes means rehabilitation, does express something important, it is about how a community should respond to those who have offended, and the responsibilities a community has towards them. They doubt if these practices can be appropriately valued if reduced to private transactions, and quoting Michael Sandel talk of "the moral limits of markets," i.e. that rehabilitation is not a product to be bought and sold. That means the provider, in this case the CRCs are doing nothing more than selling a product. Again, these arguments are additional salvos in the debate about the private sector's involvement in the public sector and a further example of an attack on neo liberalism.

The opposing argument is that a product is indeed being sold, and this is a form of rehabilitation, which may not be as of old, but is rehabilitation nonetheless. What is important is not who is doing the selling but the product itself. Accordingly a distinction needs to be made between a service and a public service. Those who see it as a service would include that group of service users I spoke with who cared little about the employers of the Probation Service. What mattered to them was the quality of the person they had to deal with. Was he/she a good or bad Probation Officer? That means was he/she fair minded, just, and able to provide help? In a situation where almost all the power was on the side of the Probation Officer, somewhat naturally those on the other side, the unequal side, were likely to be concerned with the users of that power. Their experiences told them that some officers were to be trusted and some not. That is to say some officers were fair and just in the way they made decisions, could be trusted about what was told to them, were considerate in their outlook and used information to the service users advantage. Others were not, and these were dangerous and untrustworthy. This is a less sophisticated argument than those opposed to the use of the private sector but is relevant nonetheless. To these service users rehabilitation was a negotiated provision, which came from a service by the individual probation officer.

The second of the demands placed on the CRCs is to develop a range of other services which involves specific interventions, which can be inserted into a court order. It is about opening up the markets, a question which was put to those giving evidence to the House of Commons Justice Committee. Their answers were often dispiriting.

They saw the larger companies as being more successful, and they noted that the smaller organisations seem to have struggled (Q 119). Those giving evidence thought there were two major problems, the first was that only the large companies were prepared to take on the demands of opening up the markets, the smaller companies preferring to avoid the risks. The second is that most of the services that reduce reoffending, such as those relating to housing, mental health, addiction, etc. lie outside the scope and control of the CRCs.[28] There is nothing new here; the wonder is it wasn't recognised before. What this means is that the CRCs are reluctant to step outside the rather narrow confines of traditional areas of practice thereby suggesting the prospects for opening up the markets are slim.[29]

I want to give two examples of the ways in which CRCs have failed to open up the market. The first is through Rehabilitation Activity Requirement or RARs as they are called. RARs can be inserted into a Community Order or Suspended Sentence Order. They require an offender "to comply with any instructions given by the responsible officer to attend appointments or participate in activities or both." RARs were introduced under the Offender Rehabilitation Act 2014 and came into operation in 2015, i.e. before privatisation. The precise activity can be determined at the time of the sentence or sometime later following a more in depth assessment. An activity can be of any duration from less than one hour up to one day according to the length of the session. The problem for the CRCs is that RARs have become less popular.[30]

RARs permit a wide range of activities to be included in the order, and as such are a key indicator of the strength of the range of services the government expects will be provided in the privatisation programme. New services were expected to appear, the expectation being there would be a flourishing of new activities, all encouraged by a payment scheme which would promote new developments. What we know of RARs is only from HM Inspectorate of Probation; of which there are two reports.[31] Those Inspectorate Reports show that the expected increase has not happened. In fact the opposite has occurred. HM Inspectorate of Probation said that having started with enthusiasm the CRCs are not now commissioning the full range of specialist services that are needed to make a difference to people with particular problems.[32] It said a good range of services should be available to cover diverse needs but it found a limited range of services available.[33]

Payback is another of those services that can be attached to the Community Order. Payback largely involves selected offenders doing unpaid work, and as such has a punitive element alongside a more robust demand to make recompense. Prior to 2018 unpaid work was the most frequently imposed requirement of a community sentence. It remains a popular provision second only to RARs with over 60,000 such requirements made annually. There are other schemes such as programmes to address domestic violence, or substance abuse, but RARs and Payback are the most often used.[34]

Done well, unpaid work is an important adjunct to a Community Order; although whether it reduces offending remains to be seen. Views differ about its rehabilitative potential. Also, it is time consuming for those running the programme, involving high staff ratios and considerable financial resources. Reports suggest, that like RARs it is often not done well. Comments from the Probation Inspectorate show that "only 1 in 5 placements were tailored to suit offenders," and there is "little integration with other probation work." These are mixed with other comments on community programmes; such as "enforcement is lax" or "too often the managers responsible have too little influence over the offender management of those subject to the requirement."[35] Or again, it appears there were failures to make sufficient progress in delivering activities due to ineffective management and others resulting from poor IT services, the latter necessary if the schemes were to operate smoothly.[36] All seem to agree, including those giving evidence to the House of Commons Committee, that the problem goes back to the initial contracts which they say were poorly produced by the Ministry of Justice when it rushed the initial assessments.

CRCs were introduced into the privatisation programme in the belief that they would introduce competition and thereby develop new ways of working. They would supposedly introduce effectiveness and value for money. Or, according to the Minister for Justice: "This competition will deliver real value for money for the hardworking taxpayer and ensure we get the best in the business when it comes to rehabilitation offenders."[37] Expectations were high but results have been poor. Critics were not surprised; they saw the whole process as providing nothing more than an opportunity for a bonanza for the private sector. And they ask, did the government really believe that privatisation would open up the market, and money would be saved with offenders rehabilitated by simply expecting the CRCs to develop new ways of working? If so, there must be an increasing level of disappointment in government circles as to how things have turned out.

3. A "payment by Results" incentive to pay for reductions in reoffending

The third requirement is "Payment by Results" or PbR as it is usually called. PbR has been used extensively in government departments, mainly in the Department of Health, but also in the Department of Work and Pensions as part of its work programme. It is not unique to Britain, it is used in varying forms in some countries in Europe, North America, and Australasia. In Britain it began in a limited way in 2004 but was developed and refined in 2007. PbR is the most complex of the five listed features, and unsurprisingly, equally controversial. Chris Grayling is a key supporter of PbR. He inherited from one of his predecessors Ken Clarke the wish or aim to "provide a world first – a system where we only pay for results by a diverse range of providers from all sectors."[38] Grayling also promoted the view that this was a new way of looking at the criminal justice system, and that where he was leading others would follow.

PbR is becoming an increasingly common commissioning model throughout the public sector in Britain, where, according to the Audit Office, there were over 50 schemes currently operating (in 2015), involving at least £15bn of public money. Again, according to the Audit Office there is not sufficient evidence to draw firm conclusions as to whether PBR is effective, but there are a number of reviews which show where the key learning points exist.[39]

Picking one's way through PbR is difficult. Although relatively straightforward in principle, it is complex in detail. The basic principle is thus: payments by results operates according to the rehabilitation outcomes that are to be achieved. "If CRCs deliver more they will be paid more. If they fail, the money will be paid back to the government." This is the government's mantra, and of course at one level is persuasively simple. Except, of course, it is far from that, as others have found elsewhere.

A warning from the Audit Office sets out some of the pit falls and some of the dangers:

> PbR offers value for money (but) these contracts are hard to get right which generates a risk and cost for commissioners. PbR potentially offers benefits such as innovative solutions to intractable problems. If it can deliver these benefits then the increased risk and cost may be justified, but this requires credible evidence. Without such evidence then commissioners may be using this mechanism in circumstances to which it is ill suited to the detriment of value for money.[40]

There are other warnings. The first is a general warning. "PbR is not suited to all Government services." And this is the main point: "it is most likely to succeed if the operating environment has certain features, for example where results can be measured and attributed to provider interventions." Moreover, "if applied inappropriately then there is a risk that the service quality or value for money may be undermined."[41]

Was this perhaps prescient as far as probation is concerned? The results thus far suggest it might have been. The government's aim was to provide a structure that offered the right balance between provider incentives and financial risk transfer. The Audit Office further warned

> Commissioners must understand providers costs in order to create a payment mechanism that offers an incentive to achieve the desired outcomes. If the payment is found to be too high the taxpayer pays too much, if too low providers may not bid for contracts.[42]

Perhaps another prescient.

PbR involves one minor and two major features. The minor one is *Fee for use;* that is to say fees are paid to cover work done for other parties, i.e. where NPS commissions services for its own high risk offenders. This is the least important of the basic structure and likely to produce the smallest payments, details of which are set out in a paper by the Ministry of Justice, the Procurement, Payment Mechanism.[43]

The second feature, a major one, is *Fee for services*, or FFS. This is paid for mandated activities that deliver the sentence of the court, but FFS also includes licence conditions on discharge from prison. The key components are:

1. FFS is primarily paid to mandated activities that deliver the sentence of the court and licenced conditions as specified in the contracts. Providers are free to determine their costs and operating models for the delivery of these services.
2. FFS includes the delivery of community orders and suspended sentence requirements including RARs as well as licence and suspended sentence conditions, and Through The Gate services for offenders upon reception and discharge from custody.
3. FFS is a fixed annual payment paid in 12 monthly instalments monthly in arrears for the delivery of services against the predicted WAV for the coming year.[44]

In other words, fees are paid for the satisfactory completion of activities with offenders, with additional payments for sentence type and length. There is an annual payment, and additional payments made monthly which are weighted for sentence type and length of sentence.

Fees are also triggered by reductions in offending. There are binary and frequency matrix in PbR which work as follows. The binary is about reoffending where payment is made where offending stops. It simply means success or failure is defined solely by overall reconviction rates against a cohort of offenders. The frequency matrix measures success in terms of the number of times an offender reoffends (i.e. is reconvicted). There is also a "hurdle" which must be achieved if payments are to be made.

There are 8 aspects to this:

1. PbR is paid based on a binary metric (reoffending rate. i.e. the percentage of offenders in a cohort that reoffend) and a frequency metric (the frequency of reoffending i.e. the number of reoffences per reoffender).
2. Offenders are allocated to a provider and grouped in quarterly cohorts for that binary metric.

3. Payments on the binary metric will only be made for achieving statistically significant reductions in reoffending. Deductions are applied to FFS for underperforming (i.e. increasing the rate of reoffending beyond a statistically significant point) whereas higher payments are made for further improvements in reducing rates of reoffending.
4. Annual top up payments will be available in the binary metric for statistically significant improvements against annualised targets.
5. The offenders allocated to providers will be grouped in annual cohorts for the frequency metric.
6. There is a "hurdle" set at the binary reoffending baseline which must be achieved in order for any payment to be made on the frequency metric.
7. Payment on the frequency metric will be made if there is any reduction in reoffending provided the binary hurdle is passed, and deductions applied for any increase in reoffending.
8. There will be significant financial deductions in the FFS and/or termination right for MoJ for large or repeated increases in reoffending rates.

The practical effect is that fees are paid after two years, based on scaled payments of up to £4,000 for each offender who desists, and a further payment of £1,000 for each offence avoided, based on a scale of expected reoffending.

The Ministry of Justice said in May 2013[45] that the key feature of their proposed payment structure was the "Fee for Service" element. This guaranteed certain activities being delivered – these might include attending a drug abuse course, or literacy classes, or whatever was thought necessary for the offender's rehabilitation. However further payments would be made for a reduction in reoffending. So, providers would be rewarded with other payments when they "achieve complete desistance from crime for at least 12 months."[46]

However payments will also be adjusted according to the total number of re-offences committed by a cohort of offenders. The aim here is for providers to be incentivised not to neglect the most difficult offenders and those that have already reoffended, i.e to avoid so called "parking." Payments are made according to the rehabilitative outcomes that are achieved. So for providers to be paid in full they will need to achieve a sufficient reduction in the number of offenders returning to crime as well as reduce the volume of reoffending by those offenders for which they are responsible.[47]

The emphasis throughout is that results will trigger payments. Results are what matters, and results are measured by a reduction in reoffending. That of course raises the basic question; what is meant by a result; it was after all one of the warnings of the Audit Office. In criminal justice a result is difficult to define, for in criminal justice the unit of measurement is elusive; it is not about what someone has done, but what is not done, i.e. in this case, not reoffended. Chris Grayling further complicates matters by insisting on talking of "reoffending" but as said earlier no one knows what that is. "Reconviction" is better, but this is also difficult to measure.

Results of course depend on data, but obtaining data in criminal justice is far from straightforward. Consider PbR as it applies to the health service, which is a good example of a service where PbR has been applied, and with some measure of success, for at one level obtaining data within say, a hospital setting, is more straightforward. Yet even here there are a range of difficulties which need to be overcome. I want to look at two areas of data collection, how data are identified and how outcomes are established.

When used in hospitals, PbR begins when a patient enters the hospital and ends when the patient is discharged, or seen as an outpatient. The hospital is then paid for the treatment. The commissioning service is the NHS and the providers are the hospital services. As a data driven service within the health service PbR relies on three building blocks to provide the data. They are a classification system, a currency, and a costing information system. A classification system captures the data concerning a patient, such as diagnosis and treatment, and the data can then be produced in a standardised format. A currency is a group of diagnostic codes put together to make the system more workable. So, for example in the hospital setting there are over 26,000 separate diagnostic conditions, a currency merely groups them into more manageable categories. Finally, costing information is required which is based on a tariff, which is set nationally – for example, the tariff for a hip operation is set at a certain level and differs from that for say, cardiac arrest. Adjustments are made for longer or shorter periods of stay, and types of drugs required. So, the system works as follows; the patient enters hospital, is given treatment, the patient's notes are coded, these are sent to the patient activity system (PAS), treatment is then costed, the data are sent to the Department of Health who submits them to the Commission for Payment.[48]

A major and obvious difference between the hospital setting and criminal justice relates to the way the data is identified and collected and a result produced. In the criminal justice system there is no simple classification system, no easy currency, but an elusive costing information system. In PbR as it applies to the hospital, data are identified and collected according to specific recorded events, i.e. notably when the patient leaves hospital. Not so in criminal justice. In the hospital setting leaving the hospital marks the point at which a result is identified, in the probation system it is also at the end of the supervision period, but here the similarities end; in the hospital setting a result occurs when the patient is discharged, i.e. a factual event relatively straightforward and able to identify. A result in criminal justice is when the offender is rehabilitated, i.e. not having committed further offences. That is to say a result in one system means an active event, in the other system it means the opposite.

There are other differences. In the hospital data comes from specific hospital events recorded by the hospital on each patient. In criminal justice obtaining the data is dependent on securing information about a criminal conviction, which is itself dependent on numerous variables, such as police activity, police recording, CPS decisions, and so on. Sometimes reconvictions are based on contingencies, some of which are simply on levels of police activity, or being in the wrong place at the wrong time. They are also recorded on the Police National Computer, which is notorious for the quality of its recording practices. This is partly due to the methods of recording, but also on the difficulties posed by the offenders themselves. Offenders give misinformation, move to different parts of the country, and avoid identification. Carol Hedderman says simply tracing an offender's criminal history on the Police National Computer can be a rather hit or miss affair. She says a recent check by the Ministry of Justice found that about one in ten offenders could not be found when name, date of birth, and gender were used as identifiers.[49] If then an offender cannot be traced how do we interpret this? Is a success when there is no further evidence of reoffending, or is this a failure?

Yet even in the hospital setting things are not always straightforward. In a study I carried out of compulsory admissions to mental hospitals[50] we found enormous differences in recording practices and interpretation. One hospital recorded separate admissions if the patient was moved to a different ward, another recorded separate admissions if the patient went out for a single home visit, and another used a different diagnostic classification than elsewhere. We found the most valid diagnoses came from those hospitals who did not use IT systems but simply recorded data in a notebook. So it seems with PbR in the hospitals. The Audit Commission's Report[51] also spoke of errors in classification in their hospital data, of 7.5% in 2011/12 – albeit a fall from 9.1% in 2004 but substantial errors nonetheless. These errors led to a mixture of over and under payment with a slight bias toward overpayment. Another Commission Report[52] also found errors similar to those in our research; that is to say there was no consistency in recording practices within and between hospitals. Some patients who stayed in hospital for less than 24 hours were recorded as "in patients," others similarly placed as "out patients." Clearly if this level of error occurred in a hospital setting how much more in the criminal justice system?

There is also the problem of establishing outcomes, or rather determining who is responsible for outcomes – sometimes called attribution. This was the second of the Audit Commission's warnings. In the hospital, attribution of outcomes are clear – the consultant would usually be attributed to these. In criminal justice outcomes can often depend less on services provided by the criminal justice setting, more on other organisations doing similar or associated work. For example, research currently taking place in Vancouver shows a remarkable link between prosecutions for offending and data on health, the hypothesis being that an improvement in health facilities will lead to a reduction in offending. How could this be transferred to PbR? Or take a more immediate example: assume a person appears before the court, is sentenced to a period of imprisonment, and is homeless. On his release he is later provided with accommodation by some organisation and his reoffending stops. Or again, a young woman appears before the court, and is sentenced to a Community Order. She has lost her job when she appears before the court, but in a short time a friend finds her further employment and her offending stops. In these cases who is responsible for the fall in reconvictions? The authority providing accommodation, the friend, or was it the Criminal Justice System as a result of the courts passing a certain sentence? Then to complicate matters further, where multiple providers achieve an outcome, as with those CRCs where more than one company works together, who is then responsible?

The problem goes deeper than this and concerns the question of measuring and recording qualitative issues. Wendy Fitzgibbon makes the point that binary calculations to reoffending do not include factors such as issues of risk of serious harm to self or include mental health problems.[53] She thinks there will be an increasing disincentive to measure and include these qualitative aspects and "to adapt a PbR model to measure such qualitative issues … is not methodologically impossible but would create delays in the measurement of outcomes."

There is of course always a larger dimension to the question of outcomes, that is to ask: are failures or successes due to the providers whose task it is to undertake the work in hand, or to the commissioners whose task it was to produce the appropriate contract? If the former then they should amend their working practices, if the latter they should amend the contracts. In this case it is too early to say where such faults may lie, and it is an impossible question to ask although when things go wrong, as they well might, expect a blame culture to erupt.

The basis of PbR was always about saving money. That being so the aim is to obviate various tactics that can be used by providers to achieve results which are ways of exploiting the system to advantage. They are common to all PbR systems. "Parking" involves deliberately neglecting those with more barriers to be successful and require more expensive attention, whilst "gaming" is where high risk offenders are passed onto the state by the CRCs. "Creaming" is where priorities are given to those who are considered to be easier, cheaper, and more likely to be successful. These effectively translate to overpayments by the commissioners for any given outcome and for individuals. Given that providers receive payments based on successful periods of offending – or rather the lack of it – there is a central tension between commissioners and providers and about how best to deal with them. The problem arises in all PbR contracts, including those on the Welfare to Work programme for the long term unemployed, where in this case there are nine payment groups designed to deal with these. It seems they are still not successful.[54] Taken all together, PbR becomes a quagmire through which commissioners and providers must navigate.

Should PbR have been used in criminal justice and is it successful? At this stage it is difficult to give an answer to either question. It may be too early to assess whether it is an appropriate mechanism for criminal justice, or whether it was another of those untried and untested experiments developed by the Coalition Government to be part of their austerity programme. It goes back to those earlier criticisms that there was little or no planning, no pilot schemes and no way of knowing whether it would be successful. It also goes back to other earlier criticisms that criminal justice generally, and probation specifically, is not an area on which new and favoured solutions can be simply transposed; criminal justice and probation are too complex for that. The government's expectation with PbR was to believe that a system which had operated elsewhere in the public sector could be readily introduced in criminal justice with few considerations of the complexities involved.

The obvious question is, what effect has PbR had on the financial position of the CRCs? From what we know many CRCs are in financial difficulty, but the evidence is difficult to obtain. We know nothing about how much CRCs are paid, which payments are being made and which outcomes are being assessed. These financial details are regarded as commercially sensitive and outside the public domain. Nor do we know how much privatisation is costing, or what, if any, are the savings and losses. We know that the government has had to make additional payments. As 80% of the probation budget is made up of wages and related matters are the savings to come from a reduction in staff?

We know that *"Fee for Use"* covers work done by other parties, with estimates being circulated that this will cost about £24m for the year in 2015/16. We know too that *Fee for Service* is paid in full if CRCs achieve the required service levels, the most heavily weighted where offenders, usually on release from prison, but also from the courts, actually complete various courses or requirements. And we know that *Fee for Service* also involves an annual payment paid in 12 equal instalments, monthly in arrears, where payment is worked out at the end of each year, with a clawback available for the commissioners if the providers fail to meet the targets. Also, we know there is a predicted baseline range weighted for sentence and length which providers must compete against. Finally, we know that deductions are also made for failure to deliver results from court orders. Yet we do not know the details of these costs and payments.

Questions about costs were asked at the outset but answers were rarely given. Lord Ramsbotham was scathing on costings, or rather the lack of them, when the programme was first introduced. In the Foreward to *Transforming Rehabilitation*, the Justice Secretary had optimistically said "Through the savings we make we will extend rehabilitation support to those on short term sentences …." This prompted a reply from Lord Ramsbotham, doubting whether legislation had ever been able to guarantee the consistent availability and affordability of the money and the people required to produce that support? But more important he also asked in that same debate, "What is the Governments estimate of the costs of providing a rehabilitative service to offenders released from custodial sentences of less than 12 months, and how much are they looking to recover through competition?"[55] Unfortunately there was no reply.

A similar question was asked by the House of Commons Justice Committee in 2014. It noted that the Ministry of Justice had high expectations of what can be achieved in the way of efficiency savings, "through contracting out the management of low and medium offenders," but said "we have been unable to determine whether sufficient funding is in place on the limited information the Government has provided."[56] In May 2017 the new Justice Secretary David Lidington adjusted the amounts paid to the contractors by about 10%, which amounted to another £22m. He said; "We have adjusted the CRCs' contracts to reflect more accurately the cost of providing critical front-line services" – this as a "result of unforeseen challenges following the splitting of the service." He gave no further details.[57]

In August 2017 *Private Eye* reported on a huge bailout operation of payments that were 10 times the £22m already given. It gave details of a bailout payment of £277m to the companies running what *Private Eye* called "Britain's failing private probation companies." In late July

2017 the money was paid, but not announced to either MPs or the public. *Private Eye* said payment was made for failures in the service. What was particularly interesting was that *Private Eye* gained this information by a circuitous route. It found it by scouring through more than 20 notices in a Supplement of the *Official Journal of the European Union*. It found also that in many cases ex-prisoners were interviewed over the telephone rather than in person.[58] David Lidington said of this, that these were the "challenges that were unseen."[59] On the 23rd March 2017 *The Guardian* reported that the private companies, which provide 50% of probation services in England and Wales, have confirmed they will consider leaving if the Ministry of Justice fails to deliver improvements. Interserve and MTC Novo, with contracts worth £15m, told the House of Commons Justice Committee that their finances are unsustainable. "Our work is going up, our payment is going down," said the Director of Interserve.

Was there a deliberate attempt to hide the information or was something else afoot? *Private Eye* certainly thinks it was deliberate.[60] It is difficult not to draw certain conclusions from the *Private Eye* announcements, the obvious being that there was a certain amount of subterfuge about the payments, which confirmed certain deeply held suspicions about the overall cost of the exercise. To talk of "unforseen challenges" merely confirms the point made above, that the government was wrong not to pilot the project, and worse still not to cost it. And all this to the fury of those working in the Probation Service before privatisation, where funding was difficult and extra funding almost impossible

The National Audit Office was asked to examine the financial position of the CRCs. It asked three questions; why did the Ministry adjust the contracts, how were the adjustments made, and what are the financial implications of those adjustments? Its conclusions were not surprising in the light of some of the leaks and statements made earlier, namely that the volumes of activity for which the CRCs are paid is well below the levels expected, and the numbers of offenders supervised has increased. In the first quarter of 2017/18 the volume of work was down from between 16% and 48%, and the numbers supervised up by 20%. The Ministry paid an extra £42m over the costs of the contracts, and without this extra funding CRCs said they would not have maintained a required level of service. Fixed costs for the CRCs increased by more than 20%, largely because bidders overestimated their ability to reduce costs.[61]

We were told that there would be sufficient savings to pay for the supervision of offenders released from prison, i.e. those who were part of the newly formed Through The Gate services, funded largely by a reduction in offending (see Chapter 5). Chris Grayling said that returns for both parties, commissioner and provider, will come later, although initially costs will be high. That, he said, was to be expected as setting up the schemes will be expensive. He also said we should not be dismayed about these early costs, they will be reduced later and it will all be worth it.[62] The privatisation programme with PbR at its centre will, he said, rehabilitate offenders, do so at less cost to the Exchequer, and in a manner by which the CRCs will get a return on their investment. These predictions, it seems, will have to be revised.

Staffing levels are also being scrutinised. In evidence to the House of Commons Justice Committee on *Transforming Rehabilitation*, Ben Priestly from UNISON said he struggles to know how many staff work for CRCs, what work they are doing, and what qualifications they have. Ian Lawrence from NAPO said staff reductions were estimated to be around 26%, but in some cases as high as 50%.[63] Accordingly, it is not possible to know how the CRCs are paying to collect data, determine outcomes, or paying staff. But it seems systemic failings are beginning to have a direct effect on staffing levels and profits. *Private Eye* also reports on a conversation a reporter had with the Justice Minister Sam Gyimah, who was asked of the numbers of Probation Officers before and after sell off. He said he had "no idea."[64] P*rivate Eye* then conducted its own assessment and found for the year 2015–2016 the CRCs had cut staff by 1,886, or 20% of the total. The most were by Sodexo, whose six probation services had staff cuts of 45%. Northumbria was the highest area, with cuts of 54%. Interserve had cuts of 22%, Working Links had cuts of 9%, and others by 8%. Reports also show that Sodexo, MTC Novo, and Ingus paid out £14m in redundancy payments. It was not clear which staffing levels had the most cuts, Probation Officers, Clerical Officers, or others? It seems the private sector was not producing that expected "value for money," nor receiving that windfall of profits originally expected.[65] Reality has appeared, with matters more complicated than that which can be reduced to political polemic or soundbites.

The point was made in this and the previous chapter that it was never going to be easy or straightforward to transfer public work to the private sector, especially for an institution as complex as probation. The modern commissioning provider model grossly over-simplifies the situation by reducing the work of probation to outputs and results. The CRCs have found things more difficult to manage than was expected. Similarly, adding services from the prisons has also proven to be difficult. Many such difficulties pre date TR. For example, the Offender Management model introduced decades earlier had never worked, and Probation Officers who worked within the prison setting were never fully assimilated. Many found the prison environment incompatible, and were themselves treated with suspicion. There have also been extra difficulties in administering probation services in rural areas. There are too few reporting centres making supervision difficult, and expensive, points summarised by Glenys Stacey who said, "Owners of CRCs ambitions to remodel services have found probation difficult to reconfigure and re-engineer. Delivering probation services is much more difficult than it appears, particularly in prisons and in rural areas."[66]

An additional defect is the poor quality of IT services the CRCs inherited, described by one very senior figure as "halted and sticky." For decades IT services within the Probation Service have been regarded as "unfit for purpose," with little done to update them. To those working in probation it comes as no surprise to see that the CRCs have found the IT services poor, the surprise is that they had not been noticed before. (When the Probation Service was merged with the Prison Service the problems were clear; the services had separate IT systems.) Poor quality IT services restricts communications and makes reporting additionally difficult. TR did not create these problems, but it may have made them worse. Given the current state of IT services in probation it will be a number of years before they reach a sufficient standard. The Public Accounts Committee in their Report in March 2018 thought it "unacceptable that almost half way through their 7 year contract the CRCs were still unable to link their IT systems to HM Prison and Probation services."[67]

Some work volumes which were based on assumptions about the sentencing practices of the courts have not been sustained. Sentencing practices have changed; this has meant a reduction in some orders which attract higher payments and an increase in those which attract the lower ones. The suspicion is that the decrease in the use of some orders is part of a wider problem about the relationship with the Probation Service and the courts. Under privatisation the contact with the courts is more tenuous, assisted by a corresponding reduction in full length written reports, some of which would have recommended the use of the higher paid activities. The courts, it seems, have less confidence in the Probation Service because they have less contact with probation staff. That has led to a greater unwillingness to sentence offenders to the more extensive orders. The Public Accounts Committee in June 2016 said "Reports to the Courts vary in quality, with written reports much better than reports presented orally. Some court staff had not received sufficient training and did not know enough about the work offered by CRCs."[68] So, whilst it would be easy to blame the CRCs for certain failures, it is less easy to blame them for changes to sentencing practices

How to assess the overall picture? There is no doubt the PbR scheme is not working, or at least needs additional government support. This was the view of the House of Commons Public Accounts Committee.[69] It appears that CRCs will be increasingly vulnerable through the PbR of their contracts. They are unlikely to meet their frequency targets or their overall offending targets. Was this a problem for the commissioners who failed to produce adequate PBR programme, or the providers who misunderstood what was required? According to the National Audit Office, it was the providers. The NAO reported (in 2017) that the volume of activity CRCs are paid for was well below levels anticipated when the contracts were let, and the numbers of offenders supervised has increased. The NAO said in the first quarter of 2017 the volume of activity was less than originally anticipated with the numbers supervised by CRCs up by 20%. This has led to a reduction in the amount paid under PbR for the duration of the contracts from £3.7bn to £2.1bn. Projected losses from 2016 to 2022 are £443m if the contracts are not changed. Clearly, an unsustainable position.

The Public Accounts Committee in their inquiry into the CRCs contracts were told that the CRCs encountered "unforeseen challenges," a polite way of saying that things were going seriously wrong. There were three of these so called "challenges." The first was that the number of cases referred to the CRCs were lower than expected – the figure the Public Accounts Committee were given were that in 2015 they were between 8%–34%, and in 2017 between 16% and 48%. Second that CRCs were expected to bring down costs with a decrease in volume. This has not happened. And finally, as said earlier the courts were imposing fewer specialist programmes. When it was suggested that the extra money was a way of "bailing out the CRCs," the answer was "not bailing" but "adjusting contracts to meet the facts."[70] That adjustment involves a further £342m. No wonder it was said to the Public Accounts Committee "if we were starting again we probably would have made the contracts less complicated,"[71] and it could be added that perhaps it would have helped if they were based on better information and more piloting.

No wonder the Public Accounts Committee (2018) wanted to know what the taxpayer was getting back for this extra commitment.

Notes

1. Ministry of Justice (2013) *Transforming Rehabilitation: a revolution in the way we treat offenders.* (Cm 8517).
2. Ministry of Justice. (2013) Transforming offenders: a strategy for reform. Response to consultation. (CP 9R. 16/2013). (Cm 8619).
3. Ibid. P. 44.
4. Private Sector Finance or PFI which elsewhere is called private–public-partnerships, are contracted to complete and manage public projects. The theoretical justification is that the private sector is more efficient at delivering and managing infrastructure projects than the state. However, a National Audit Office report has said PFI contracts are between 2% and 4% mere expensive. See *Financial Times* 17th January 2018 "UK finance watchdog exposes lost PFI billions."
5. House of Commons (2016) Transforming probation: a revolution in the way we manage offenders. HC 484. (Cm 8517).
6. From the Ministry of Justice (2012) Punishment and reform: effective community sentences. (CP (R) 20/2016).
7. Letter to *The Guardian* (5 November 2013).
8. Ministry of Justice (2011) Probation service wins excellence award (October). Pg. 7.

9 Quoted in NAPO (2011) Breaking up probation and the Excellence Award (1st November).
10 Le Vay (2016) *Competition for prisons: public or private*. Policy Press. Pg. 145 and 151.
11 House of Lords Debates, 2nd Reading, 20th May 2013. Col. 661
12 Quoted in Editorial; Grayling's Hubris. *Probation Journal*. Vol. 60, No. 4, pp. 377–382. Pg. 380.
13 Andrew Selous debate with Jenny Chapman at the Westminster Hall (25th October 2013).
14 Deering J and Feilzer M (2015) *Privatising probation*. Policy Press. Pg. 77–78.
15 Ibid. p. 77.
16 Ibid. p. 76.
17 HM Inspectorate of Probation for England and Wales (2017) Annual Report 2017. Pg. 6.
18 Deering J and Feilzer M (2015) op. cit. Pg. 72.
19 National Audit Office (2016) Report by the Controller and Auditor: Transforming Probation. (April) HC 951. Para. 3.3.
20 NAPO (2015) Briefing paper. An overview of probation services.
21 Deering J and Feilzer M (2015) op. cit. Pg. 73.
22 Le Vay (2016) op. cit. Pg. 245.
23 Deering J and Feilzer M (2015) op. cit. Pg. 72.
24 Burke L and Collett S (2015) *Delivering rehabilitation: the politics governance and control of probation*. Routledge. Pg. 12.
25 Ibid. pp. 184–186.
26 Burke L and Collett S (2016) Transforming Rehabilitation: organisational bifurcation and the end of probation as we know it. *Probation Journal*. Vol. 63, No. 2, pp. 120–135.
27 Canton R and Dominey J (2018) *Probation* (Second Edition). Routledge. Pg. 264.
28 House of Commons Justice Committee (2018) Oral Evidence on Transforming Rehabilitation. HC 482. Q 93–128(25). (30th Jan and 27th Feb). Q 121 and 128.
29 Ministry of Justice (2016) *Transforming Rehabilitation: a revolution in the way we treat offenders*.
30 HM Inspectorate of Probation for England and Wales. (2017) Annual Report 2017. Pg. 7.
31 Two reports, HM Inspectorate of Probation for England and Wales (2017) Annual Report 2017 and HM Inspectorate of Probation for England and Wales (2017) The implementation and delivery of rehabilitation activity requirements, provide the only information available.
32 HM Inspectorate of Probation for England and Wales. (2017) Annual Report. P. 6.
33 Ibid. P. 4.
34 Ibid. HM Inspectorate of Probation for England and Wales (2017) The implementation and delivery of rehabilitation activity requirements. P. 68.

35 HM Inspectorate of Probation for England and Wales (2017) Annual Report 2017. Pg. 69.
36 HM Inspectorate of Probation for England and Wales (2017) The implementation and delivery of rehabilitation activity requirements. Pg. 48.
37 Ministry of Justice (2013) *Transforming Rehabilitation: a revolution in the way we treat offenders.* Cm 8517.
38 Ministry of Justice (2011) Payment by Results, Para 23 (Oct) and Ministry of Justice (2010) Breaking the cycle: effective punishment rehabilitation and sentencing of offenders. Cm 7972. Para 23.
39 National Audit Office (2015) Outcome based payment schemes: government's use of Payment By Results. HC 86 (June).
40 Ibid. Para 16.
41 Ibid. Para 8.
42 Ibid. Para 12.
43 Ministry of Justice (2014) Procurement: Transforming Rehabilitation programme. Payment mechanism.
44 Contracts are written in such impenetrable jargon that one wonders how anyone can know what is being offered. Take for example a WAV or Weighted Annual Volume. A WAV is defined as: "A single measurement of volume based on a number of offender starts and in the case of unpaid work the sentence requirement length, and comprises differently weighted service requirements" (Ibid, para 4.1). What does it mean, and if one knew that then how much is it worth?
45 Ministry of Justice (2013) Transforming Rehabilitation. Summary of Responses. See also Ministry of Justice (2014) Procurement: Transforming Rehabilitation programme: Payment mechanisms, for a more detailed account of how and when payments are made.
46 Ibid. Para. 22.
47 Ibid.
48 The formula for the system then is as follows; Provider Income = Activity x Price x MFF. Activity consists of the codes which set the tariffs. The price is based on a tariff which is arranged according to the cost of services related to annual costs, and the MFF is unique to each organisation to reflect the expose of patients to specific features of care unique to specific parts of the country.
49 Hedderman C (2013) Payment by Results: hopes fears and evidence. *British Journal of Community Justice.* Vol. *11*, No. *2*, pp. 43–58. Pg. 47.
50 Bean P T and Nemitz T (1995) Discrepancies and inaccuracies in statistics for detained patients. *Psychiatric Bulletin.* Vol. *19*, No. *1*, pp. 28–32.
51 National Audit Office (2012) Audit Commission Report. Right data. Right Payment. The Stationery Office.
52 National Audit Office (2012) Audit Commission Report. By definition: improving data definitions and their use by the NHS. The Stationery Office.
53 Fitzgibbon W (2013) Risk and privatisation. *British Journal of Community Justice.* Vol. *11*, Nos *2–3*, pp. 87–90. Pg. 88.

54 Carter E and Whitwell A (2015) Creaming and parking in quasi-marketed welfare at work schemes. *Journal of Social Policy*. Vol. 44, No. 2, pp. 277–296.
55 Lord Ramsbotham speaking during the House of Lords Debate on the Offender Rehabilitation Bill, Second Reading, 20th May 2013. Col. 661.
56 House of Commons Justice Committee (2014) *Report on Transforming Rehabilitation programme.* HC 1004).
57 UK Government (19th July 2017) Probation reform: open letter from the Secretary of State for Justice David Lidington.
58 *Private Eye* (11–24 August 2017) World takes break. No. 1450. Pg. 7.
59 UK Government (19th July 2017) op. cit.
60 *Private Eye* (11–24 August 2017) op. cit. Pg. 7.
61 National Audit Office (2017) An investigation into changes to Community Rehabilitation Companies contracts. Press Release. 19 December 2017.
62 House of Commons Justice Committee (2014) Report on Transforming Rehabilitation programme. HC 1004.
63 House of Commons Justice Committee (2018) Oral evidence on Transforming Rehabilitation. Evidence given by Ben Priestley from UNISON and Ian Lavender from NAPO (30th January). HC 382. Q 93 and 95.
64 *Private Eye* (11–24 August 2017) op. cit. Pg. 37.
65 Ibid.
66 Stacey G (2017) Speech to Clinks Annual Conference. (2nd November).
67 House of Commons Public Accounts Committee (2018) Investigation into changes to Community Rehabilitation Companies contracts. HC 897 (March).
68 House of Commons Public Accounts Committee (2016) Transforming Rehabilitation inquiry (June 2016). Paras. 2 and 10.
69 House of Commons (2018) op. cit.
70 Ibid. Q 34 and Q 58.
71 Ibid. Q 44.

5

PRIVATISATION AT WORK

"Through The Gate" and the Probation Institute

"Through The Gate" (TTG) resettlement services is the fourth major aim listed in the previous chapter. It was directed towards tackling an entrenched problem dealing with the after care of prisoners on release. The services were introduced under the privatisation programme and operate across most prisons in England and Wales. They began on the 1st May 2015.

4. Joined up "Through The Gate" resettlement services across most prisons and the community

Under privatisation the CRCs were contracted to manage the provision of TTG services for all short term prisoners. They were mandated to manage those services regardless of whether the offender would ultimately be an NPS case, or a CRC. A short term prisoner is one serving 12 months or less. The plan is that each prisoner is to be seen at the beginning of the sentence, during the sentence, and just before release. On release offenders are expected to receive a tailored package of supervision allowing rehabilitative support to extend from custody to the community. Taylor *et al*[1] describe it in terms whereby the CRCs undertake a screening of all new prisoners within 5 days of their custodial sentence, devising and managing a resettlement plan for the duration of their custodial sentence, and then drafting a pre release resettlement plan when the individual enters the final 12 weeks of their sentence.[2] The aim is to provide this so called seamless web of service from custody to the community, producing "connected interventions."

"Through The Gate" is government's flagship policy, intended to bring about a sea change in rehabilitation and reduce offending. It extended post release supervision and support for offenders serving short term sentences who were formerly ineligible. As Chris Grayling said, "It is little wonder we have such high offending rates when you have a prisoner leaving HMP Liverpool given a travel permit to get home to the South Coast and then expected to simply get on with it."[3] Few would disagree, but introducing the programme has provided a considerable challenge to prison and probation at a time of declining budgets.[4]

There are two main features to the programme; first, that before they are released all prisoners are to be sent to resettlement prisons near their home, and second, there will be that "seamless web" of care. It is an ambitious programme where support is to be given from the point at which the offender is sentenced right through to a period of post release after care.

Resettlement services are expected to be available to all prisoners in resettlement prisons. The CRCs are contracted to make the resettlement plans, but can subcontract if they so wish. A report by the HM Prison and Probation Service described in greater detail what resettlement means: "Resettlement is where prisoners and their families receive assistance and support from the Prison and Probation Service and voluntary agencies to help them prepare for life after prison."[5] Such preparation includes attending pre release group sessions, attending drug and alcohol treatment courses where appropriate, as well as receiving help with accommodation, work, and benefits.

Resettlement prisons constitute about 80% of all prisons in England and Wales. They were established to ensure inmates are released from jail close to the areas in which they live. The prisons are grouped in regional areas. This means, with a national network of 80 or so prisons, they are organised in 21 areas, located to match the new contact areas of the CRCs under which the probation service was privatised. This is the first problem; that CRCs are not coterminous with other criminal justice agencies. Second, that making a local prison a resettlement prison confuses matters. Local prisons have a certain role to play and to add another layer of duty on them adds to the confusion. Third, it means a loss of revenue for the prisons. Under privatisation the prisons are no longer offered resettlement, services as the CRCs are now contracted to deliver those. The funding goes to the CRCs, and of course CRC staff are not employed by the prison service so there is no possibility of using them for other duties or on emergencies should they arise. Finally, it means transferring prisoners to a prison near their home prior to release. This poses considerable demands on an already overstretched prison service, particularly so for women prisoners where there are fewer prisons and greater problems of transportation.

There is also the problem about the term "resettlement." What does it mean and what are those involved in "resettlement" expected to do? It is easy to present it as something aspirational, worthwhile, and achievable, but more difficult if questions are asked about its aims and objectives. I want to explore this in some detail.

The main parts of the legislation to deal with the privatisation programme is found in the Offender Rehabilitation Act 2014. Section 2 provides for these offenders sentenced to less than two years in custody to spend the second half of their sentence subject to licence conditions in the community. Section 3 creates an innovative period of additional supervision which is added to the licence to make a total of 12 months mandatory rehabilitation after release. So, an offender sentenced to, say, three months in prison will serve half the sentence in jail, the other half on licence and the next nine months on supervision. A range of flexible requirements can be imposed during the supervision period, such as for drug treatment. Offenders who break conditions of their licence/supervision can in certain circumstances be recalled to prison, or dealt with in less severe ways. It was hoped that the same supervisor would begin supervision during the prison sentence and continue on release.

There are 6 listed duties for the CRCs:

1. Prepare a resettlement plan within 5 working days of the sentence being completed by prison staff.
2. Help prisoners find accommodation.

3. Help prisoners with employment including training.
4. Help with finance, benefits or debt.
5. Provide support for victims of domestic abuse and sex workers.
6. Undertake pre release coordination.

These duties appear on the face of it reasonably straightforward, but they hide a greater level of complexity. First and foremost, as Rob Canton and Jane Dominey say, "resettlement" implies resuming a settled life that was enjoyed before,[6] when of course that settled life rarely existed. And would a resettled offender be someone who no longer reoffends? The assumption is that it would, but it may not. Others, such as Mike Maguire, talk of different models of resettlement, such as desistance which is aimed at reducing reoffending, and of a community model which is aimed at a more inclusive approach. Maguire points to different models of resettlement rarely found in a pure form but more often representing a mixture of strategies. These might include government demands for public protection and cost savings, mixed with requests to provide ex offenders with assistance with accommodation and employment.[7] Incidentally, the Council of Europe[8] distinguish between "resettlement" and "after care." The former is defined as involving voluntary participation, and the latter as a duty of the state towards those who have completed their sentence, with all prisoners having a right to meaningful opportunities of reintegration. In the Council of Europe's terms we should be talking of "after care" rather than "resettlement."

There is nothing new in the listed duties to CRCs. For example in the 1960s the Probation Service was urged to take on a similar task, albeit offering services on a voluntary basis. This was of course in addition to all those prisoners on statutory licence. It even had its name changed to "The Probation and After Care Service." Sadly, it was not successful. Not only was it overwhelmed by the sheer numbers and their demands, but the service was under funded. It was also unpopular with probation staff. As a result prison after care stumbled on as before, except of course that in the intervening years much more was being done within the prison system itself. Courses, plans, and assistance with employment, alongside assistance with those having drug and alcohol problems are now part of a detailed and extensive prison training programme What is new in the privatisation programme is the statutory requirements imposed on short term prisoners on release, with the move from voluntary after care to statutory after care (or resettlement).

Changing to the new privatised version was, in Grayling's words, not an easy challenge, but a necessary one. The Probation Inspectorate in 2017 reminded us that our expectations should be tempered by realism. Reducing offending is difficult, success by no means readily available, and even where everything possible has been done mental illness and drug addiction can be enduring, and accommodation for former offenders increasingly hard to find. Nonetheless there now exists the political will for the step change that governments and others dearly wish to see.[9] This is welcome news for many prisoners who may now serve the latter part of their sentence near their home. The problem then and now is that too much is required, with too little funding and too little time to consider the implications. The CRCs are in the front line of this development; the question is are they equipped and capable to meet what is required? Resettlement prisons are another of those interesting aspirational ideas, but again the way they were introduced suggests there was too little planning, and too little detailed consideration necessary for such an undertaking. There is nothing new in resettlement prisons; they closely resemble Community Prisons proposed by Lord Woolf in 1991, in his report after the Strangeways prison riots, where he wanted better prospects for prisoners to maintain their links with families and communities and an enhanced role for prison officers.[10]

Notwithstanding any problems created for the prisons themselves, there are severe logistical problems involved when bringing such large numbers under supervision. Sadiq Khan, the Shadow Justice Secretary, was surely right to ask whether reality was different from rhetoric when he questioned the ability to introduce such a substantial reorganisation when there is already a shortfall of 8,000 prison places.[11] Consider the numbers involved. In the three months from 16th October to 16th December 2016 there were 267,000 offenders being supervised in the community and of these 165,000 were supervised by CRCs and 102,000 by the NPS.[12] The administration of the system is complex enough but the sheer numbers involved, entering and being discharged from prisons daily in England and Wales, makes attempts at follow up a difficult task.

Added to these are the complexities of the "resettlement needs" of the offenders themselves. Many require multiple services involving multiple agencies. Often released prisoners are homeless and accommodation difficult to find. A report by HMI Probation called on the Ministry of Justice and the Department for Communities and Local Government to recognise released prisoners as a priority need for housing.[13] I doubt this will happen. Prisoners are not likely to be a high priority in the scheme of things. What with their lack of suitable and available accommodation, together with their other needs these short term prisoners present some of the most intractable problems in the criminal justice system. Consider the following characteristics of offender populations. This taken from the Prison Reform Trust in 2011:[14]

Those having been taken into care; there were 27% compared with 2% of the general population (in my own research on street prostitutes it was 42%);

Those having been excluded from school; 49% compared to 2% of the general population;

Those having numeracy and literacy levels of 11 years or below; 65% and 48% respectively;

Those having 2 or more mental disorders; 72% of men and 70% of women;

Those having histories of hazardous drinking and drug abuse; 83% of men and 66% of men respectively.

Offenders are not a compliant work force, waiting to respond to all the help that is available. Some pose extremely difficult and complex problems. No wonder we have often failed. Sadly, the conclusion from many of the reports on the work of the CRCs providing "Through The Gate" services say that these services are still not providing the expected solution. Most suggest the problem is straightforward; the basics are simply not being provided. Many prisoners are discharged with few, if any services available to them. Too often many comments from the Probation Inspectorate make the point that "too many prisoners reached their release date without their resettlement needs having been met or even recognised."[15] A report in 2016 noted that,

> ... our concern was that Through the Gate expectations were not being given priority on the ground. Probation providers were more focussed on the more immediate demands of leading and managing wholesale change to the delivery model for all probation services. Now more than 6 months later we find little change and little delivered.[16]

Much was made of this "seamless web," to continue with the embroidery metaphor, and there are many who were hopeful about the outcome. For if successful, these plans for prison after care would be a major breakthrough. Yet the defects in the proposals were obvious from the start; there were too many offenders, requiring too many services. Unsurprisingly, the results have been less than satisfactory and in some cases condemnatory. Damaging comments have appeared in various inspection reports, such as where the NPS claim the "CRCs don't know what they are doing," or "there is no continuity," or "we send out our plans but the majority of CRCs do not read them. They are not acknowledged." Or, "Offenders did not know the name of the responsible agency or the specific individual who was to prepare them for release." Or, "Probation was perceived by many of the prisoners to be more interested in monitoring and surveillance than providing support."[17]

Other criticisms were made by Glenys Stacey, the Inspector of Probation. In her Submission to the Public Accounts Committee she said. "Some people now under supervision do not meet with their Probation Officers face to face. Instead they are supervised by telephone calls every 6 weeks or so with some CRCs planning for biometric monitoring systems."[18] Later, in a speech to the Westminster Legal Forum she said:

> Given that the provision of Through the Gate services was a significant driver for the changes introduced under *Transforming Rehabilitation* it was discouraging ... to find that over two thirds released from prison had not received enough help pre release in relation to accommodation employment or finances.[19]

These failings were a huge disappointment. Who was to blame? The commissioners or the providers? Was too much being asked, or too little being done to make the system work? Glenys Stacey seems more concerned to blame the providers, and in doing so is less pessimistic in the long term about the outcome. Or rather, she is less fatalistic, hoping for some improvement. In that speech to the Westminster legal Policy Forum (7th November 2017) she says "There is a strong evidence base to show the quality of the relationship between an individual and his probation officer is paramount." The implication here is that with better provisions, i.e. more and better trained staff, improvement can be made and services improved. It may be a question of time, but she thinks change is possible. (Yet I wonder what the Inspectors would have said had inspections been made of the prison after care services provided in the late 1960s. I suspect the results would have been strikingly similar.)

Yet interestingly enough the service users themselves did not complain about the service they received from the CRCs. About one year after privatisation 77% of those surveyed by the National Audit Office said they had not noticed any change in the overall service.[20] Dissatisfactions, such as they were, turned out to be the same as always; too little help with housing, and too little help with employment. (How many times have Probation Officers heard that oft stated lament "With a job and digs I'll be O.K.," and how rarely have Probation Officers been able to answer these requests.)

The views of service users reported by the National Audit Office were identical to those seen by me from the Nottinghamshire/Derbyshire/Lincolnshire area. I am not suggesting I saw a representative sample of users, but when asked about the impact of privatisation they all said "Nothing much has changed." Some said things were better, there were "New offices, lots of information about programmes." Others said some things were worse, "too high caseloads" being one of the criticisms most often cited. The most trenchant criticisms were reserved for those CRC officers working in prison, when,

> Before release you see a Probation Officer but not much comes of this. They simply tell you what to do and tell you to meet your offender manager on discharge. They tick boxes and make sure the

paper work is done. I don't think much of it. Doesn't do anything in prison.[21]

Or as one service user said "I've never known anyone come out of prison with a job. They'll ask about employment such as 'What do you want to do?' Then it goes back to ticking boxes." And when asked about the likely differences in approach from Probation Officers in the NPS and those in the CRCs all agreed there was no difference. Such differences as have occurred, they said, were in the quality of the officers; some were better, some were worse.

Reports by the Chief Inspector of Probation are not all condemnatory, although initially most were. Subsequent reports however, also by the Chief Inspector of Probation, suggested an uneven pattern with some areas doing good work. For example in a later report in 2017 the Inspectors said they found "exceptional practice at the CRC in Cumbria," this being "the best we have seen."[22] But this level was not sustained. In another report, in November 2017 in West Mercia, the Inspectors found the quality and assessment by that CRC to be "poor," with the CRC and the NPS needing "to improve the quality of their work."[23] In June 2017 a report focussing on longer term prisoners reached similar conclusions, perhaps even more damning. "None of the early hopes for 'Through The Gate' have been realised." It added "the gap between aspiration and reality is so great that we wonder whether there is any prospect that these services will deliver the desired impact on rates of offending."[24] This was a long way from that "seamless transition" between prison and community. In some cases there were hints of improvements. An inspection in October 2017 in Cumbria found evidence of the best probation work the HM Inspectors had seen in a CRC since they started inspecting the reshaped system three years ago. The inspectors found, "Exceptional practice at the CRC," with "The enduring values of probation and evidence based professional practice shining through in case after case."[25]

Nonetheless in the view of the Probation Inspectorate if "Through The Gate" services were removed tomorrow, the impact on the resettlement of prisoners would be negligible.[26] Report after report provided an account of a service overwhelmed by the task in hand. It was of course an uphill task faced by the CRCs to cope with the many thousands of short term prisoners released each year, making it impossible to provide a rehabilitative service for each and every one of them. Yet this is what was expected. And even if the numbers of prisoners were considerably fewer the task would still have been daunting. In fact, "Through The Gate" was a flawed concept to begin with. It required CRC officers to reduce reoffending and provide the necessary rehabilitative services for a group of prisoners, with no possible hope of it being successful.

The defects lie in the assumption under which resettlement was introduced. That is to say the expectation was a Probation Officer – CRC or otherwise – would be able to exert a rehabilitative influence through a small number of interviews and a number of follow up services on discharge. It was never going to be that simple. The first and most obvious problem is of the offenders themselves, a point made numerous times before. These offenders have a level of complexity that cannot and will not be swiftly resolved. And certainly not on the basis of the proposals introduced here. Their social and personal problems have developed over a 20 or 30 year period and are intrinsically part of their character and lifestyle. Added to these are the external obstacles faced by someone with no employment history, no settled accommodation, and often with a drug and alcohol habit. What prospects are there for employment? Probably, none, at least in the period immediately following discharge, and this of course is a key period most likely to produce reoffending. Then there is a desperate shortage of hostel accommodation – few probation hostels have been built in England and Wales since 2001 – and the housing market is in decline for the type of accommodation required by offenders. To produce a "Through The Gate" service with such a flimsy set of community provisions is nothing short of tokenism.

To provide an appropriate "Through The Gate" service much more would be required, whether in terms of finance or manpower. An effective "Through The Gate" service would be very expensive. It would require huge numbers of volunteers working with trained mentors able to provide the appropriate assistance and training. Recruiting the necessary numbers of volunteers would itself be difficult – there has never been a time when so few volunteers are being used in the criminal justice system generally, and recruiting and training new ones would take time and money. The voluntary organisations would be expected to provide the main sources of recruitment, these being the most likely organisations in which there are likely to be sufficient numbers of recruits and sufficient numbers with an understanding of criminal justice. Those doing the training could be CRC officers or from the NPS, it matters not as long as the mentors were well trained. Mentoring would also involve more than simply providing a set of "how to" type activities, it would require helping provide extensive risk assessments on each offender, and support for those at the contact point. Even the mentors would need specialist support and assistance necessary to understand and cope with the ethical problems that arise dealing with this type of offender. Without the necessary infrastructure turnover would be high and the system quickly become close to collapse.

Dealing with this type of ex prisoner requires staff who are knowledgeable and experienced within the criminal justice system. This is a programme that would require planning and care. Nor would it be available for all short term prisoners; there would need to be a selection process where only certain prisoners would be offered these rehabilitative services — there would never be enough mentors and volunteers to cope with all those discharged. A selection process would presumably be based on risk, together with an assessment of need and available facilities in the community. This might appear to undermine the very basis on which "Through The Gate" services were introduced, but that is because they were presented as a generic heuristic solution which was never likely to be achieved.

It is said that Chris Grayling was warned that his "Through The Gate" system would fail, but he chose to go ahead anyway. This and the barrage of other criticisms concerning levels of practice by CRCs working in the "Through The Gate" area can only have a damaging effect on morale. Yet the CRCs are not always at fault. As said above some of their problems were inherited and systemic; it was too much to expect sudden and dramatic improvements. Were it possible to design a new probation system, starting with a system which would include the principles under which the service would operate, follow this by introducing some feasible options, and finish by making a choice about the one that is preferred, the outcome would not resemble the Probation Service of the NPS or that inherited by the CRCs. There are too many defects. It was too much to expect and require the CRCs to be suddenly transformed into a new public service, acceptable to all, including the government and private contractors, able to deal with literally thousands of discharged prisoners annually. Probation, and the after care of ex prisoners has never been easy to understand let alone promote. To introduce a commissioning/provider model into that type of service, and expect immediate results was unrealistic. The strength of the Probation Service has always been what it represents, rather than what it is doing, and that is always likely to be a barrier to any attempt to impose a system which is dominated by inputs, outputs and results as the "Through The Gate" experiment demands.

What is rarely mentioned in a discussion of the overall scheme of things is the impact on charitable institutions with a history of working within the prison system. Rob Canton and Jane Dominey hint at this when they say that the resettlement programme fractured many existing relationships between prisons and voluntary sector organisations which had developed over time and which were suddenly brought to an abrupt end with prisoners being moved just prior to release.[27] That point was made forcibly to the Public Accounts Committee in March 2018 when in evidence to that committee it was noted a number of prisoners had received considerable support from a wide range of good third sector charitable organisations. These withdrew when statutory provisions under privatisation were introduced. "The consequence is that the richness of what is being provided is not as it was previously."[28]

We should not therefore expect sudden or dramatic changes to the reconviction rate of this group of ex prisoners, but hope for a steady decline over a selected period. Were it possible to achieve a 3% or perhaps a 5% reduction in reconvictions in a 12 month period this should be seen as a major success. Failings, such as they are with the "Through The Gate" programme, must be seen within the context of the prison system generally. Taylor *et al* blame the Commissioners saying that prisons are places of dehabilitation not rehabilitation,[29] and these reforms in *Transforming Rehabilitation* do not and cannot address that. They say that without fundamental change in the system little or nothing can be achieved by way of rehabilitation. That may be so, but the current state of the prison system, with its overcrowding, high rates of drug use, levels of violence, including suicides of inmates, has added to any inherent problems about what prisons stand for. Additional demands such as those from "Through The Gate" were always going to be of secondary importance when other more pressing problems require urgent attention. It becomes a statement of the obvious to say that "Through The Gate" must be evaluated within the context of the criminal justice system generally, and the prison system specifically. That being so it was never going to be possible to impose on the prison system extra demands without there being some ill effects, and too much to expect that a prison system with its attendant problems would simply move effortlessly forward and take on new demands. The Probation Inspectorate recognise this when they complain that prisons do not screen offenders and do not assess risks of harm, adding that "wider problems within the Prison system means prisoners rarely receive effective rehabilitation while detained."[30] The Government seems to recognise at last that the delivery of the sort of service provided under Transforming Rehabilitation was not going to work. In its publication *Strengthening probation, building confidence*[31] it said the Government recognised that in many areas Through The Gate services were not meeting expectations and too often offenders' resettlement needs were not being addressed (para 59). It thought that defects were in part the result of the funding pressures CRCs have faced since contracts were let. Hence an additional £22m per annum is to be invested so that CRCs can improve (para 60). The Government hopes this extra funding will help offenders overcome the barriers to effective resettlement (para 60). But will it? Almost certainly not. Success will cost more than that. A fully effective mentoring service alone will be more expensive let alone the costs involved making the necessary changes to the infrastructure such as housing, employment etc.

5. The Probation Institute

Turning now from a failed system to a successful one; an important feature of *Transforming Rehabilitation* has been the creation of a Probation Institute, the fifth and last of the major aims listed in the previous chapter. It was seen by some critics as an afterthought, but to others has the prospect of producing a centre of excellence. It was announced on 3rd December 2013 by Chris Grayling following a *Prospectus* in November 2013. It was officially opened on 21st March 2014 by the President of the Supreme Court, Lord Neuberger. Already established, and available for the rehabilitation sector, it is intended to support professional development, building on the probation service's considerable experience in managing offenders in the community. The expectation is that it could provide a framework for unifying the probation workforce.

The general view is that the Institute is to be welcomed, albeit long overdue. It is expected to provide professional leadership – something that has been missing hitherto – and therefore a welcome provision. The Institute has twin ambitions. They are

1. To provide professional leadership enhancing the status of probation and a context and framework for the development and support of effective practice.
2. To be a centre of excellence contributing to the setting of standards by providing an independent evidence informed view of what constitutes good practice helping to bridge the gap between research and the problems and issues facing practitioners on the ground.

The plan is that the membership will provide probation workers with a framework for training and qualification. It will be mainly for those wanting to enter the profession as well as for continuing development for those who wish to use it. It too is not without its critics, some of whom see it as another ploy by government to sweeten the privatisation proposals, but the positive side is that it is off to a good start, said by one commentator to have an independent spirit if not being independent in the financial sense.

A code of ethics has been introduced which has been universally welcomed. The code requires members of the Institute to carry an obligation to abide by the code. The first Interim Director, Sue Hall, said that practitioners and organisations are strengthened when a profession's values and ethical principles consciously guide practice and service delivery. The code is a statement that claims to reflect the Institute's core values and ethical principles and serves to underpin the probation profession helping to guide and support the work of its members. It has eight principles, which are not only of interest in themselves, but provide an important benchmark, showing how far and in what direction the Probation Service has moved these last few decades. I have selected three but do not wish to convey the others are of less importance, merely that these illustrate the point about the changes that have taken place over the years and the different emphasis now being placed on probation practice.

Principle number one from the code says: "We believe in the ability of people who have offended to change for the better and become responsible members of society." This is clarified and added to by a secondary statement which says: "Desistance from offending may take time requiring a level of patience, care and proactive engagement on the part of the worker." This is not contentious and in fact restates an age old belief in the aim of probation, which has been there since its inception.

Principle number four from the code states "We believe in the worth of probation supervision in the community based on establishing positive relationships with service users to promote their rehabilitation." The secondary statement states "Effective supervision relies on setting an environment in which sensitive issues can be explored whilst maintaining appropriate role boundaries." Again, nothing contentious here, and no difference from the one above in that it again states a basic principle of practice, albeit set in modern language. There is however a hint that modern supervision is more about controls than existed in earlier times.

Principle five from the code states "We recognise that full consideration should be given to the rights and needs of victims when planning how a service user's sentence will be managed." This is a considerable departure from those earlier times, not only because the secondary statement suggests that "restorative justice can be a useful intervention for crime victims" but because there is a recognition of the importance of the victims as such. Not only has the Probation Service been reluctant to involve itself with partnerships such as those involving restorative justice, but victims were never part of that world view – certainly not in that so called "Golden Age." This is a significant change of direction and to be welcomed accordingly.

Principles six and seven are about the importance of training and the development of knowledge through research, where in both cases the aim is to inform probation policy and practice. Re emphasising the importance of training would seem a basic requirement in any professional activity. After all training has been held as a pre requisite for good probation practice since the inter war years. To give research such importance is however new – at least compared with the late 1970s period. The lack of attention given to research results, especially those concentrating on effectiveness, has been an Achilles heel of the Probation Service for decades, although changes have taken place more recently. Its attitude to research has typically been to stand apart from it, or dismiss it as of little importance, or worse suggest it failed to examine the key variables of probation practice which were known only to practising probation officers. Recognising that research cannot be ignored is another of those substantial changes in approach for the probation service generally, and also to be welcomed.

All in all then the introduction of the Probation Institute is seen as a positive development. And ending this chapter on a positive note would suggest there are some aspects of the probation service which bode well for the future. The question however is what sort of future does it have? Will it survive, and if so in what form will that survival be? That will be the subject of the next and final chapter.

Notes

1 Taylor S, Burke L, Millings M and Ragonese E (2017) Transforming Rehabilitation during a penal crisis: a case study of Through The Gate services in a resettlement prison in England and Wales. *European Journal of Probation*. Vol. 9, No. 2, pp. 115–131.
2 Ibid. Pg. 117.
3 Travis A (4th July 2013) Grayling's prisons plan to ensure inmates are released close to home. *The Guardian*. The legislation was more than just for the probation service. It was "to make provision about the release of offenders, to make provision about the extension period for extended sentences prisoners, to make provision about community orders and suspended sentence orders and for connected purposes."
4 Canton R and Dominey J (2018) *Probation* (Second Edition). Routledge. P. 233
5 HM Prison and HM Probation Services for England and Wales (2017) Joint Report. (5th April).
6 Canton R and Dominey J (2018) op. cit. Pg. 234.
7 Maguire M (2007) The resettlement of ex prisoners. In Gelsthorpe L and Morgan R (eds) *Handbook of probation*. Willan Publishing. Pp. 398–424.
8 Quoted in Canton R and Dominey J (2018) op. cit. p. 235.
9 HM Inspectorate of Probation for England and Wales (2016) An inspection of Through The Gate resettlement services for the short term prisoners.
10 Lord Woolf (1991) *The Woolf Report. A summary of the main findings and recommendations of the inquiry into prison disturbances*. There were 12 recommendations. Those referenced here are from recommendation 9 and 2 respectively.
11 Quoted in Travis A (2013) op. cit.
12 Stacey G (2017) Probation services: getting back on track. Portel Lecture. Institute of Probation 2nd Annual Conference. Sheffield. (June).
13 HM Inspectorate of Probation for England and Wales (2017) An inspection of Through The Gate resettlement services for discharged prisoners serving 12 months or more. (June).

14 Prison Reform Trust (2011) *Prison Factfile*.
15 HM Inspectorate of Probation for England and Wales (2016) An inspection of Through The Gate services for short term prisoners. P. 7.
16 Ibid.
17 These quotes are taken from HM Inspectorate of Probation (2017) Annual Report 2017 and Stacey G (2017) op. cit.
18 Stacey G (2016) Submission to the Public Accounts Committee. Transforming Rehabilitation Inquiry. (27th June 2016).
19 These quotes are from Stacey G (2017) Next steps in probation reform in England and Wales. Speech to the Westminster Legal Forum, and her Submission to the Public Accounts Committee (27 June 2016). Pg. 15.
20 National Audit Office (2016) Report by the Controller and Auditor General. Transforming Rehabilitation. (April). Para. 3.17.
21 Anon. Pers. Com.
22 HM Inspectorate of Probation for England and Wales (2017) Quality impact inspection. The effectiveness of probation in Cumbria. (5th October). An Early Day Motion in the House of Commons (Number 52) on the 26 June 2017 expressed similar concerns. It called on the Government to review the performance of the CRCs and NPS as well as the TR programme. The Motion had 11 signatories, none from the Government. Faced with these criticisms it is difficult to see the way ahead, unless and until there are massive changes to the way "Through The Gate" operates.
23 HM Inspectorate of Probation for England and Wales (2017) Quality and impact assessment inspection. The effectiveness of probation work in West Mercia.
24 HM Inspectorate of Probation for England and Wales. (2017) (June) op. cit.
25 Stacey G (2017) Press release. 5th October 2017.
26 Stacey G (2017) Next steps in probation reform in England and Wales. Speech to the Westminster Legal Forum. (7th November). An area which was most disappointing was the lack of human contact between some service users and their probation staff, leading to the so-called "telephone culture." Glynis Stacey the Chief Inspector said "There is a strong evidence base to show the quality of the relationship between and individual and his probation officer is paramount." She adds that this being so it is disappointing therefore that "some cases are transferred between probation workers routinely. And some people now under probation supervision do not meet with their Probation Officers face to face. Instead they are supervised by telephone calls every six weeks or so with some CRCs planning for biometric monitoring system (p. 2).
27 Canton R and Dominey J (2018) op. cit. Pg. 235.
28 House of Commons Public Accounts Committee (2018) Investigation into changes to Community Rehabilitation contracts. HC 897. (March). Q 29.
29 Taylor S *et al* (2017) op. cit.
30 HM Inspectorate of Probation for England and Wales (2017) The implementation and delivery of rehabilitation activity requirements. Pg. 57.
31 Ministry of Justice (2018) *Strengthening probation, building confidence*, Cm 9613.

6

THE FUTURE OF PROBATION

There was something inexorable in the government's thrust towards privatisation, but there was nothing inevitable about it. Different decisions could have been made, different programmes offered, and a different Probation Service would have emerged. But there was certainly something inexorable in the build-up through that long drawn out process described in Chapter 2, and the emerging neo liberal view, exemplified by Carter, that governments must promote systems which are effective, efficient, and offer value for money.

At the time of writing (July 2018) the new system has been in place about four years. Is it working? The answer seems to be it is not. Report after report have produced a catalogue of failings, all describing an unsatisfactory situation. The first Annual Report of the newly formed HM Inspectorate of Probation concluded that "regrettably, none of the Government's aspirations for *Transforming Rehabilitation* have been met in any meaningful sense."[1] A later report reached similar conclusions. A reprint in June 2018 was even more aware of some of the failings of the privatised system.[2] The overall picture therefore is not good, and this after so many changes, so much effort, and so many promises for the future.

If this pattern continues changes will be required, yet the government earlier said it restricted the amount or extent of change it can make whether it will keep to this is another matter. Even so, in 2014 the Ministry of Justice imposed a time limit restricting widespread change of 10 years from the date of privatisation. Of course, no government can bind its successor, but future governments might believe they should accept these impositions. (The time limit was also imposed and justified in order to encourage the private sector to bid for contracts. This so called "Poison Pill" is not unique to probation. It was introduced alongside the privatisation of the railways, where train operating companies had similar time limits included in their franchises.) Grayling also said 10 years were required to put right a failed system; failed in the sense that the reconviction rates for ex-prisoners on short term sentences had for a long time remained stubbornly high. He also pointed out that he inherited a "deeply entrenched problem," requiring a radical and sustained effort to resolve it. He was correct therefore to say that we should not expect immediate success. And of course, were these reforms to be successful, it would be a massive achievement.

What are the likely outcomes? As things stand (in 2018) the Government has recognised that the CRCs are in financial difficulty and by implication that PbR is the most vulnerable of the current features of privatisation. It has pledged a further £22m per annum to offset deficiencies, and agreed with current providers to end existing contracts earlier than anticipated – two years earlier in fact. The plan is to explore with stakeholders and the market how to put in place more effective delivery arrangements and wider system improvements beyond 2020 (p. 6). The hope of many was that there would be a return of the private sector to public ownership, which would involve transferring all controls back to the NPS. This would be welcomed by those such as Lord Ramsbotham might not welcome the disruption, and the financial loss involved, but would certainly welcome returning the Probation Service to public ownership. He in particular sees it as the only course of action, and says it cannot survive otherwise (Lord Ramsbotham, Pers. Com)[3]. Yet this, according to the latest Government Report is not likely to happen. The Minister for Justice said "I believe there is strength in the mixed market approach" or again, "We will explore with the market how in future we could establish a more effective commercial framework which better takes account of changes in demand for probation and ensures that providers are adequately paid."[4]

A likely outcome is that a single contractor might fail and/or ask to step down from the contract. If so, this would also pose serious problems for the Government, leaving a number of offenders without supervision and raising questions of public safety. In which case the Government would have to choose between different options. Either, it could offer other providers the possibility of stepping in and taking over the caseload or it could provide a patch up service covering defects by extra funding. The latter would seem more likely, this being the type of recovery provided to the railways when one of the newly privatised train services failed. Extra resources were simply thrown at the failed system, allowing some sort of compromised solution to be reached. To some extent this has already happened with the extra money for the CRCs.

There is a wider question about finding ways of improving the working practices of the two groups and avoid that 'chasm' said to be growing between them, especially where one is in a more secure occupational setting than the other. It must also recognise that there are now two separate services, undertaking separate tasks with different structures and aims. The division of labour, especially where it involves only one sector working in the courts – incidentally, the Probation Service's traditional power base – can only exacerbate the situation, and induce a sense of superiority in one group. Being part of a second class service will not sit well with many CRC Probation Officers, and being excluded from the courts makes it difficult for the courts to know and understand what they do. Some repair work is needed here, to give the CRC worker a greater measure of importance, and show that the division between the CRCs and the NPS is not reducing incentives and the quality of work.

The Government believed that privatisation would 'open up the market' and produce an innovative system of new providers. This too has not happened. Nor is there any likelihood it will, given the current method of funding, the practices of the CRCs and the way the courts sentence. CRCs contracts were based on assumptions about the use of the more expensive services, and assumed a greater level of income than has been the case. Adjustments have been made to the CRCs contracts with the expectation that additional revenue will offset this loss and encourage a more active approach, and in the latest Report the stated aim is to work more with voluntary sector organisations, but it is doubtful if this will produce the required changes, including the introduction of new projects. Again, it does not bode well for the future; it means the Government will be required to continue providing additional financial support to offset the loss for a long while to come.

A most serious failure has been "Through The Gate" services, where report after report found these to be missing targets, and not providing the necessary facilities for the rehabilitation of offenders. "That is the nub of it; too little meaningful work," said one Inspectorate Report.[5] As these services were the main justification for privatisation, it is a serious blow to supporters to recognise their failings. At best it can be said Through The Gate was a valiant attempt at providing a solution to an outstandingly difficult problem, but at worse they turn out to be a costly failure. There were too many obstacles; too many prisoners, with too many personal and social problems, with too few outside opportunities to make it a success. The only solution is to recast the programme, preferably along the lines suggested in Chapter 5, i.e. with a specialised mentoring/volunteer service for selected prisoners.

But what if things improve? There is of course the possibility that the programme will become successful and survive. This should not be discounted, so that were desistance from crime to be achieved within the time span suggested by Chris Grayling, there is every likelihood the current system will remain. That is to say there would still be an NPS dealing with high risk offenders, the CRCs dealing with medium and low risk. PbR would remain as the main method by which privatisation is sustained, and Through The Gate services still operational. There might be minor changes, certain deficiencies might be identified and dealt with accordingly, but the general structure would stay as it is. It is also possible that the privatisation of probation might set precedents for other privatisation programmes in criminal justice, perhaps in the police, the prison service, and the courts. Indeed, when asked by members of the House of Commons Justice Committee if *Transforming Rehabilitation* has a future those giving evidence said "yes." (There were exceptions. The NAPO representative said "no.") They added that there needs to be opportunities to reassess, but no radical changes were required (Q 145. 27th Feb 2018).[6]

So, in spite of all predictions of failure, there remains a possibility the existing structure will remain, at least in some recognisable form. This does not mean it will be trouble free, but occasional successes have produced an optimistic note. When Dame Glenys Stacey, the Chief Inspector of Probation, was also asked (in June 2017) if the existing service will survive, her answer was also a positive "Yes." She added, however, that survival was not guaranteed.[7] In a later speech (19th September 2017) to the Criminal Justice Management Council,[8] she asked "*Can probation services deliver what we all want and support?*" And again, she was positive.

In the first Speech Dame Glenys Stacey set out 5 conditions necessary for survival. The first is that governments must address the immediate funding issues, and do so in ways that do not fall foul of existing contract law. The second is that CRCs must be placed on stable financial footing. So, although existing contracts will constrain activities, demands for more money by the private sector will have to be met. This may come as a surprise, given that numerous critics and commentators said the CRCs were being overpaid, and that privatisation was a bonanza for the private companies. Now, we are told there is a shortage of funding, with demands for more supported by HM Inspectorate of Probation.

The third condition required for survival suggested by Dame Glenys Stacey is that there must be sufficient financial inducements and rewards to produce good quality work. That is to say, governments must be clear about what they expect of Probation Services, and as a corollary, CRCs and the NPS must be clear they must improve standards. Having been freed of the constraints of National Standards she thought the service could innovate. She made no suggestions as to how this should be, but innovations might include using more volunteers, and unpaid work. Also, the government should have a strategy for deciding how probation services are delivered.

The fourth condition made by Dame Glenys Stacey is about what constitutes a good service, and her fifth and final condition is that there is a greater need for incentivisation to produce that good quality work. These latter conditions include important questions of value and principle. For example, there remains much confusion about what a good service should look like, and what is "good quality work." No one seems to know, yet we make demands of the NPS and the CRCs that they need to improve.

Some of these five conditions can be met without making wholesale changes. Governments can decide how much money to spend on a privatised service and allocate funds accordingly. It does appear that the voluntary societies attached to the main financial corporations are doing the least well financially, and if so a financial correction is required. For the third condition the Inspectorate will doubtless offer suggestions, many of which could include a greater input from the voluntary agencies. The final two conditions however concern basic questions about the sort of Probation Service we might want, that is, if we want one at all. They require more attention and are sufficiently important to be dealt with in more detail. Accordingly, I want to give over the remainder of this chapter to these, hoping to arrive at some conclusions about the sort of Probation Service we might want, now and for the future.

I want to concentrate on three areas: first the governance of the service; then the work to be undertaken by a Probation Service; and finally, its ethos. The three selected areas are part of a wider debate which I think should begin about the type of Probation Service we want for the future. They have grown out of the narrative on privatisation discussed in Chapters 4 and 5 above, but of course there are other matters, equally important, which for the present have to be set aside. Some of the following discussion applies to both sides of the divide, private and public sectors, others apply to one side only. All are about the future of probation.

1. The governance of the service including CRCs

First the governance of the service, which concerns the NPS and the CRCs. The current position is thus.

CRCs operate at Level 1 on the privatisation scale, as private companies with shareholders. And as private companies CRCs are of course regulated by the 2007 Companies Act. They are also inspected by HM Inspectorate of Probation. Those CRCs which are voluntary organisations are governed by their own statutes and regulations. All staff in the CRCs are employed by the CRCs, but according to TUPE Rrgulations (see also Chapter 1). The CRCs are usually headed by a Chief Officer with four or five Assistant Chief Officers reporting directly to the Chief. Assistant Chiefs usually represent a geographical area. The CRC management structure is similar to that of the earlier probation trusts. It is unlikely there will be changes to that structure, or the governance of the CRCs at least in the immediate future, except perhaps greater controls granted to the Chief Officers.

Things are different for the NPS. The Secretary of State is at the apex, and below is HMPPS, which is an Executive Agency of government responsible for Prisons and Youth Custody estate, as well as the NPS. The NPS is divided into seven geographical divisions, each headed by a director. These seven geographical divisions are coterminous with a group of CRCs which means the NPS works alongside several CRCs in their divisional areas, the exception being Wales which has its own NPS area and CRCs, but now offender management on low and medium risk offenders is to be transferred to the NPS in Wales. A public sector NPS and 21 privately owned companies deliver the probation services across England and Wales. Staff in the NPS and the CRCs are called "Probation Officers" but their employing authority differs, adding to the complexity of any discussion on governance. The NPS is part of an Executive Agency of HMPPS but the CRCs are free to structure and organise themselves.

The current situation for the NPS is unsatisfactory.[9] An obvious effect of being tied into the HMPPS is that the National Probation Service has no clear voice. Moreover, it is linked with an organisation with a poor reputation for sound management. The immediate problem then is to remove the National Probation Service from the HMPPS and provide it with a more satisfactory form of governance. In doing so the aim would be to provide it with a structure capable of meeting change, whether in the private or public sectors. I am assuming that in the short term few changes will be made, and the service generally will remain divided between public (NPS) and private (CRC). I suspect there is no appetite for another upheaval, or for more dramatic changes, at least in the short term. The longer term might be different.

The expectation therefore is that the NPS and CRCs will work alongside each other at least in the immediate future. There may be changes to working practices, such as improving contacts between the NPS and CRCs, making them more efficient, more flexible and more effective. They might also include improving management skills, and updating facilities such as IT. They could certainly provide better office services, such as removing open plan offices, which are common, and provide others which allow the necessary privacy for sensitive and difficult conversations to take place. In the longer term changes could be made which would strengthen the service, notably in its contact with government.

It was said in Chapter 3 that a major weakness of the Probation Service generally in the build up to privatisation was the lack of direct representation to government. That needs to be put right. We are of course talking only of the NPS at this stage.

Lord Ramsbotham has suggested the following model which I think has considerable merit.

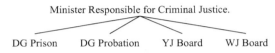

Minister Responsible for Criminal Justice.

DG Prison   DG Probation   YJ Board   WJ Board

Note: DG is Director General; YJ is Youth Justice; and WJ is Women's Justice.

Beneath each main section would be the various sub offices. So, for example beneath the Director General for Prisons would be the directorate for each type of prison, including Young Offenders and a Directorate for Foreign Nationals. There would also be Planning Officers. For NPS probation, there would be chief officers for the regions, including a Directorate for Prison After Care alongside a Directorate for Community Sentences. The aim of such a structure is to allow various sections to be fully represented, and in a manner where an organisation such as probation is on an equal footing with say, prison or youth justice or women's services.

A further aim of this governance model is to regionalise the structure. It is similar to that proposed by Lord Woolf in his report on the Strangeways Prison riots[10] and picked up in the 1991 White Paper on *Prisons, Custody Care and Justice*.[11] Regional managers for the Probation Service would work with the courts, police, health, education, and local government to provide comprehensive treatment programmes for offenders. Prisons and probation would have the same aim. "It is our duty to help all those committed by the Courts to live useful and law abiding lives." HMPPS would be abolished. Boundaries would be realigned, where for some extraordinary reason Chris Grayling organised them to fit those of the Department of Work and Pensions, as opposed to those of criminal justice.[12]

A weakness of the pre privatisation form of governance was that there was no direct access to the Minister. It was a weakness then, and is a weakness now. Lord Ramsbotham's model remedies this. Absence of a direct contact with government permitted, if not hastened the predicament in which he service finds itself. A structure of this type and format would help place the service in a more secure position.

To some extent the formation of the National Probation Service in 2001 moved it in the direction suggested above. There was a National Director accountable with direct access to the Minister. Unfortunately, that Probation Service was rather quickly merged with the Prison Service, into NOMS, as it was then, and as said earlier, widely recognised as a disaster for the Probation Service, it being overwhelmed by a larger more dominating Prison Service. Hence, the model suggested above which involves a separation from the prison system but with access to the Minister.

Lord Ramsbotham's model also takes account of the Youth Justice Board and the Women's Justice Board giving them equal status with the Prison and Probation Service. These organisations have been part of NOMS and are now included in HMPPS. Their remit lies outside the scope of this book.

At the local level Lord Ramsbotham suggests the aim would be for each regional directorate to have access to the main directorate, who represents local interests – "local" in this sense means regional, and not local as existed with numerous small local probation areas. The model of the earlier probation trusts seems appropriate here. These regional directorates would work with other groups of similar interest. These would be the police, the courts, and the prisons making Lord Woolf's concepts of community prisons more a reality. The danger of course is that taking too much account of local concerns blurs the wider picture.

The problem of course is the CRCs. They are private companies having contractual agreements with the government to provide certain services. They made their bids on the basis that they would deliver those services and are expected to proceed accordingly. As such their working practices do not fit easily into the Ramsbotham model. Nor do they fit easily into an NPS scheme of things; CRCs are contracted to deliver a set of services supported by a plethora of providers and subcontractors all working at different projects in different local circumstances. As long as there are private companies it is not possible to have a unified service. In fact, the presence of CRCs means we are further from a national service than ever before. It might be possible to have some uniformity about the way CRCs operate, linking their practices to the way the NPS manage their caseloads, but to move beyond this, towards a unified service, new contracts would have to be negotiated and a specification inserted that "all CRCs deliver their services in a certain way." This, however, would prove difficult. The original contracts were offered on the basis that the government wanted new ways of thinking and new ways of working, the intention being to separate further the CRCs from the NPS. That separation now exists and shows itself in numerous forms of practice, not the least that the CRCs have moved away from face to face contact with offenders.

Of course, this should not stop the NPS moving towards the Ramsbotham model. The Ramsbotham model would make the NPS independent yet provide opportunities to work with other agencies at the central and local level, and to have a clear vision about its aims and objectives. It also provides an opportunity for the service to realign itself with others similarly inclined, and have its views represented at the highest level. But it still means there are two separate probation services, which will remain so as long as the CRCs remain.

Other models have been suggested, but there are not as comprehensive and appealing as that suggested above, and they face the same problems with the CRCs, i.e. the CRCs are private companies and cannot be merged with the NPS. NAPO has offered one such model, but this is about where control should lie rather than provide details of governance. It offers three possibilities.

1. Mayoral Model. This has produced some interest in London but not everywhere has mayors, and NAPO says those that do are still establishing themselves.
2. Police and Crime Commissioners Model. But, says NAPO, the PCCs have no political credibility with the public and little visibility. Nor do they have any known capacity from running anything as complicated as this.
3. Local authorities to take over responsibility. But, NAPO believes LAs are struggling financially and evidence from Social Services

would suggest that they are a risky offload for any Minister looking to devolve risk and blame.

NAPO's conclusion is that none of these options are fully formed. This is not a reason to dismiss them, but NAPO says each have defects. In evidence to the House of Commons Justice Committee on *Transforming Rehabilitation* (27th February 2018) it was noted that in Manchester responsibility for most of criminal justice has already been devolved to the mayor. It was too early to say if it was working.[13]

The most favoured of NAPO's three models would be that involving the Police and Crime Commissioners. It has the advantage of being nationwide, offering a democratic appeal, with commissioners able to exercise influence in government. Yet NAPO accepts the PCCs have no experience dealing with or running a criminal justice agency other than the police. There would be no direct contact with ministers, but the objectives of the Police and Crime Commissioners are similar to that of a Probation Service, which is to promote safer communities and provide protection to the residents.

Included in the current governance of the Probation Service is an active inspectorate, and this should be retained. A Probation Inspectorate began as far back as 1936, although not put on a statutory footing until the Criminal Justice Act 1991. It was subsequently amended by the Criminal Justice and Services Act 2000. The functions of the inspectorate are set out under Sections 6 and 7 of that Act, which include specifying the numbers of members of the inspectorate and its duties. The inspectorate is to report to the Secretary of State on the effectiveness of the service.

An influential and active inspectorate is essential. It is necessary for upholding standards, giving advice to ministers, identifying good and bad practice, driving up performance, and safeguarding the interests of the offenders. The reports by the current inspectorate, especially those since privatisation, have identified weaknesses and failures in the system and have become central to the subsequent debates. Currently the inspectorate concentrates on performance. It measures and focuses on tasks completed, rather than seek justification for those tasks. Hopefully the inspectorate will go beyond this and spend more time seeking justifications.

There is a strong argument for a closer partnership with the police. The police serve local communities and are increasingly concerned with the supervision of and decisions about offenders within a community. The police and probation have overlapping tasks as with the sex offender register, and the Sexual Offences Prevention Orders, as well as responsibility for victims, reparation, bail hostels, etc. However, any strategic and operational alignment with the police must be defined within the context of a loose arrangement. The experience of the merger with NOMS should be a powerful reminder of the dangers of being too closely linked with a larger more powerful collaborator.

Getting the governance right is important for a newly aligned Probation Service. Good governance is a necessary condition of a good service. The model suggested here would go some way to provide the necessary framework for the second feature of a good service; i.e. the work to be undertaken.

2. The work to be undertaken

In 2001 the Home Office set out what it saw as the aims of a Probation Service. They were to reduce reoffending, to provide the proper punishment of offenders in the community, to ensure offender's awareness of the effects of their crime on its victims and the public, and the rehabilitation of offenders.[14] They do not however say how these should be undertaken or which areas of work should be included.

Yet it seems axiomatic that certain basic tasks exist within all criminal justice systems which need attention. They cover certain areas of work which may not fit easily into a unified system, but all require attention. One or a number of organisations could cover them, but ideally a transformed probation system would be the most appropriate. We can call this service the "Probation and Parole Service" or "Community Justice Service" if the term "probation" is not acceptable, or perhaps something else; the name doesn't matter. What matters is to be clear about what should be done.

I suggest there are five areas to be covered. They are;

Supervision of offenders on Community Orders.
Supervision of offenders on prison licence, including parole.

Preparation of selected offenders for release from custody.
Preparation of reports for the courts.
Care for victims of crime.

All governments must accept that an organisation is required capable of working in the courts, in the community, and in the prisons. It must be an organisation of sufficient flexibility to be comfortable in these situations. Preferably, it would be a single organisation; a dystopian vision would be of multiple organisations competing with each other, working in similar or adjacent occupational and geographical areas. This would not only repeat many of the failings of the existing system but add to them by introducing new complexities.

Consider the first and second of these five areas to be covered, the supervision of offenders in the community, and the supervision of offenders on licence including parole. Presumably, there is no dispute that there will continue to be some form of community penalties, and of course parole is one of them, but for the moment leave parole aside. Again, call these orders what you will. They may be Community Orders, Community Rehabilitation Orders, or Suspended Sentence Orders, or something altogether new. Again, the name for the moment is unimportant. All require the actions of a supervising authority. The new orders would involve the supervision of offenders, and may also involve Levels 2 and 3 types of privatisation such as "tagging," or substance abuse therapies provided by outside agencies. The orders may be short term, say lasting only a few weeks, or longer, but again their length is not what matters. The important point is that offenders will require supervision with sanctions and breach proceedings available where conditions are not met. For the moment also leave aside the question of whether supervision will be undertaken by the NPS or the CRCS. These questions can be dealt with later.

Supervision involves restrictions on liberty, on movement and association. These restrictions require justification simply because they limit the freedom of actions or activity. For the criminal justice system that justification comes from the law and through the courts. That leaves us with questions about the nature of the supervision; do we want a system whereby enforcement is regarded as an end in itself, or is the aim to achieve something more positive? If the first, then we can make do with reporting systems which involve checking into an electronic device, and do without human contact. If the second, then we require something more personal.

The evidence, such as there is, suggests that human contact is to be preferred. NAPO in a different context, talks of staff having more purposeful and better focussed contact with offenders when they were allowed to exercise their professional judgement in deciding how to work with each individual.[15] Alison Leibling in her discussion of the privatisation of prisons suggests there are good reasons for thinking that organisations that aims to improve standards of behaviour are best staffed by altruistically orientated workers.[16] Peter Raynor and Maurice Vanstone are equally certain about the merits of human contact and of the use of skilled staff. "Skilled probation staff are up to twice as effective as less skilled staff in reducing offending."[17]

The Chief Inspector of Probation is also firmly opposed to mechanical reporting systems, believing that a close forthcoming relationship between an individual and their Probation Officer is key to effective supervision. She laments the fact that some offenders do not meet with their Probation Officer face to face, but are supervised using telephone calls every six weeks or so, and supervision is often by junior professional staff often carrying caseloads of 200 or more: "I find it inexplicable that under the banner of innovation these developments were allowed".[18] There may of course be a place for reporting systems which involve mechanical methods of recording, as an adjunct perhaps to human intervention, but the inspectorate believe that every assessment of them makes clear they do less well.

So, if human contact is necessary, the question then is about the nature of that contact. Supervision involves, enforcement, and compliance – enforcement implies control, and compliance implies agreement, which means the person under supervision agrees to abide by the conditions of the order. How much emphasis then should be given to one rather than the other? All offenders under supervision require some measure of enforcement and will in return be expected to offer some measure of compliance. This will of course vary according to the conditions and type of order, parole for example requiring more enforcement and compliance than others.[19] What then should be the balance?

Here I want to concentrate on the enforcement side looking more at the rules and the implications of those rules.

Privatisation, and the build up to privatisation, has been more concerned with rules and enforcement than with compliance. Changes from SNOP onwards have emphasised enforcement, moving towards increasing levels of record keeping and risk management.[20] National Standards tightened up procedures, initially for selected community penalties, but later for the Probation Order itself. Action is now to be taken when an offender fails to comply with certain conditions of post release supervision including licence, when no acceptable explanation is forthcoming. In detail that means a warning is to be issued, or appropriate action taken within two hours for emergency cases, and within 24 hours for non emergency cases. These requirements limit discretion and innovation. Perhaps slowly, it has become recognised that imposing more demands does not always produce better results. Rather, an increase in demands often leads to an increase in bureaucracy and an over reliance on process. These then become more important than delivering outcomes.

The history of enforcement in the Probation Service has been lengthy and complex. It has traditionally been of lesser interest to serving Probation Officers, they being more concerned with compliance. Yet some form of enforcement has always been a feature of probation supervision, whether through the traditional Probation Order, the Community Order, or parole. There was always a requirement to report to a Probation Officer "as and when so directed" – although reporting itself may have provided a convenient opportunity for therapy. Failure to report may have led to enforcement, even if not always acted upon. Over the years enforcement has allowed for fewer options on the serving officers. It is now a problem, and a problem not always of the Probation Service's making.

No one doubts the importance of record keeping, of the allocation of cases, of planning risk management and enforcing the courts' sentencing practices. But might it be that managerial considerations have overtaken the traditional aims of probation? If so, what are the possible solutions? The answers would seem to lie in basic questions about the aims of enforcement, such as what rules are required and what should be the level of enforcement when such rules are broken?

An answer to the first question is clear; the aims of enforcement is desistance from crime. And desistance in this context as stated by Tony Bottoms[21] occurs when one of the following conditions are met. First, when there is no further offending within a specified time period – that could be longer than the length of this sentence or the period of licence. Second, when there is no further offending on this sentence, but there would have been had a different sentence been given. Third, when there has been successful completion of this sentence or period of licence, and finally, where there has been a reduction in say, alcohol consumption or drug abuse, or changes in the drugs used which are less addictive than before. The first and third of these conditions are straightforward, but the second and fourth are more complicated. In the second it is impossible to determine whether an alternative sentence would have been a success or failure. The final one is akin to Bentham's view that a reduced level of criminality may be only a partial success, but can be counted a success where drug use occurs in a reduced form or in the types of drugs taken. Common to all four conditions is that determining levels or rates of desistance is always problematic, but that does not affect the overall aims.

What is less straightforward are the rules themselves; their nature and extent. How restrictive should they be and what are to be the penalties if and when they are broken? An obvious point to begin is to assert that the rules themselves should be clear and unequivocal, a precept again derived from Bentham, who derided "Judge & Co" for the power they gained from imprecise rules. Imprecision makes for an uncomfortable position for those on the receiving end, hence the need for clarity. Beyond this matters are more difficult. Questions about the nature of the rules suggest that supervision becomes troublesome, to use one of David Faulkner's terms if the rules make demands which are beyond the offender's capacity to cope.[22] Supervision then becomes pointless and oppressive. Rules therefore should be sufficient to ensure the offender moves into a settled way of life and not add to the punishment already inflicted. It does mean however that the offender does not commit offences, and reports to the supervisor as required, but beyond that the rules imposed ought to be a matter for individual cases. So for example, one offender with a drug problem might be required to attend a rehab clinic, and another with convictions for domestic violence to attend a similar training programme. Given the likelihood of failure (drug rehab for example has a notoriously low success rate) being unable or unwilling to succeed ought not to be a matter for immediate and automatic enforcement. In doing so it would mean acting beyond the capacity of the offender.

The impact of strict levels of enforcement have produced some troubling results, sometimes paradoxically producing more criminality. Take for example parole supervision where increasingly large numbers are recalled to prison, not for committing further offences but for non compliance with parole restrictions. The figures for the 12 months up to 31st March 2017 show that 47% of offenders on parole were recalled for non compliance (out of 21,721), a number so large as to make up a significant proportion of the prison population.[23] The fear is that we in England and Wales might be following the American pattern where increasing numbers of offenders are in prison, not for their immediate offence but for failing or breaking conditions of a community type order. Mike Maguire and Peter Raynor were concerned in 2006 about the likely impact of the mandatory supervision of short term prisoners, and its impact on the prison population as a result of having to enforce thousands of technical breaches of supervision requirements. They said we will not be promoting desistance but a revolving door of detention. Similarly, the Prison Reform Trust says the number of people recalled to custody following their release has increased dramatically since changes were made under *Transforming Rehabilitation* and introduced in prisons in February 2015. The recall population increased by over 1,000 in 2 years and at the end of March 2017 stood at 6,554.[24] Already we have in Britain, under the Criminal Justice Act 2003 (under Section 8) powers to imprison offenders for breach of a Community Order even when the original offence was not punishable by imprisonment.

The high rate of recall means that either the requirements of parole are beyond the capacity of many parolees, or the regulations too restrictive. If, as the parole figures suggest, restrictions are beyond the capabilities of many offenders the solution is to choose between having fewer offenders on parole, or a softening of parole conditions. It seems we cannot have both.

A possible way forward is to permit a greater measure of interpretation. Rules that are fixed and inflexible appear to have led to unintended results which are to the detriment of all concerned. Might there now be a case for giving greater levels of discretion to the rule enforcer. This is not to suggest a return to idiosyncratic enforcement. David Faulkner believes the Golden Age where "advise, assist and befriend" dominated led to "sloppy" practice in that no one knew or cared much about the rules, or indeed about the effectiveness or success of the operation.[25] The result was careless enforcement, which he sees as equally sloppy. It was this lack of interest in reoffending that upset governments and contributed to the introduction of National Standards, and in part was responsible for the probation service's current position.

What is interesting however is that there seems little positive association between "tough" enforcement and reduced levels of reconviction. Offenders exposed to tough enforcement regimes have reconviction rates that are no different from those in more lenient areas.[26] It appears that tough or strict enforcement can lead to offender subversion, and opposition to the organisation's aims. All of which gives further support to the suggestion that a greater latitude is needed. Might it be that offenders under probation supervision are largely inured to threats of breach, but they may be more affected by a softer approach to enforcement.

I might add a minor complication about the rules themselves and their levels of importance and ask; is breaking some rules more blameworthy than breaking others? Governments do not always recognise differences, and have sought to require similar levels of enforcement for all types of rules. For example, all offenders are required to keep appointments, and report as instructed. This is the same for an offender who is also a substance misuser and required to be drug tested, or if convicted for domestic violence then not to approach certain premises. The tricky question is about whether an offender who breaks a reporting requirement should be dealt with in the same way as an offender who fails a drug test, or returns to an otherwise restricted geographical area? Is breaking one rule more or less blameworthy than breaking another? No one seems to know, but is a question worth asking.

Which raise another question; what constitutes failure? Is it determined by the breach rate, or the commission of further offences? Or both, and is one more important than the other? The muddle we get ourselves into is largely due to our inability to sort out basic questions such as these. Assume for example there are two Probation Officers with identical caseloads, yet one has a higher rate of breach proceedings. Is one a better officer than the other, "better" in the sense that a higher breach rate means imposing a stricter level of enforcement, or does it mean the officer has less control? Or perhaps the officer with the lower rate has greater level of compliance, or imposes less strict levels of enforcement? These are not aimless questions. George Mair and Rob Canton[27] also ask; is the government to expect higher or lower rates of breach proceedings when deciding on efficiency and effectiveness? Does a higher rate mean the system is working better, or should it be the other way round? Again, no one seems to know.

Whatever the nature of the rules they must be underpinned by an agreed moral justification. That moral justification must come from the law which itself gives legitimacy to the rules. Legitimacy is a *sine qua non* of all sets of rules within criminal justice. And by legitimacy I mean that which is acceptable according to those rules. Tony Bottoms draws attention to this when he notes the importance of legitimacy in the ordinary encounters between staff and offenders in prisons which can have crucial implications for the nature of the power relations involved. Also, legitimacy provides validity to the claims by staff to justify their authority.[28] Bottoms notes that in prisons the prisoners perceptions as to whether the staff are acting fairly are highly correlated with their assessments of the prison regime. Legitimacy requires office holders to act fairly. Widespread injustice provokes disorder, said Bottoms. That means the question is what do prisoners see of the behaviour of their custodians? Is it justifiable, comprehensive, consistent, and thereby fair? Or alternatively, unwarranted, arbitrary and capricious?[29]

Legitimacy is necessary in probation for a number of reasons, one of which is due to the imbalance of power between the enforcers and the enforced. The Probation Officer–offender relationship is complicated, in that it involves a curious imbalance of power, mixed with a wish to be of assistance. It takes place in circumstances where the offender has little choice about who should be the officer, and of the officer's aims and intentions. That was why the government was correct to impose limitations on professional actions, but incorrect to have moved too far in that direction. It is also why legitimacy should be an integral part of all Probation Officer's training programmes. All power relations stand in need of legitimacy and the Probation Service is no exception.

Legitimacy is a means of promoting active cooperation between Probation Officer and offender. A good Probation Officer is fair, that is one who makes clear the rules, and the conditions under which rule breaking will be enforced. It involves conveying a message that enforcement will only occur under certain circumstances, and these are set out in advance. Fairness is the opposite to caprice, which involves creating a climate of certainty. Fairness is universally welcomed, that is why it is important for an organisation such as probation to give it prominence in probation practice.

There are certain necessary conditions that help promote legitimacy. One is to publicly reward and compliment offenders on obeying the rules. Clearly people respond when complimented on their responsive behaviour. The American Drug Courts have something to offer here where one of their central tenets is to publicly reward offenders for good behaviour and for achieving goals set by the court. Judges will offer rewards – they may be nothing more than a public announcement that standards have been met, or that appointments have been kept – but coming direct from a key authority figure has considerable impact. "I've never had a judge say that to me before," is a typical response to such a public pronouncement and compliment, and the effect is often such that further compliance is guaranteed. More than that there is often now a willingness to please. Of course the effect may not last but in some cases the impact can be huge and compliance secured. I am not suggesting judges in Britain slavishly follow the American pattern, but I am suggesting that encouragement be introduced into a future set of rules regarding supervision.

What we are seeking then is a system which involves a level of human contact with appropriate levels of enforcement for those who resist. Handling this apparent dichotomy between enforcement and compliance has been the bedrock of the Probation Service for decades, there is nothing unusual here. What is difficult is agreeing on that level of enforcement is required, so that one is not unbalanced by the other. The government had increasingly moved towards enforcement, perhaps because it interpreted the public mood as moving also in that direction (promoting popular punitiveness) or perhaps it saw increased enforcement as a means of reducing crime and thereby reducing costs. If it did then it was mistaken, and the time is now right for a change of direction.

The third of the five requirements is preparing selected offenders for release from custody. For these purposes the area of interest is in "Through The Gate" services. The aim was to operate these services on the basis that prison staff remain responsible for the immediate needs of all offenders in custody, and the CRCs develop a resettlement plan which will be available to prison staff to assist with case management. These resettlement services may include helping offenders find accommodation, providing family support, financial advice, and support for domestic abuse. The CRCs can also provide "mentoring support" where required. In some prisons there will be a CRC host/lead provider responsible for completing resettlement plans and in others, called "shared adult male prisons" there will be a host/lead provider and a "host," the latter being in contact with the prisoners home.

Such were the aims and aspirations. The reality, as I said in Chapter 4, has turned out to be different. To repeat the points made there; report after report has called into question the activities of the CRCs in prison, suggesting that the resettlement plans did not robustly address the most urgent resettlement needs.[30] Through The Gate services did not, and could not cope with the enormous numbers of discharged prisoners, nor were the services offered adequate to meet the needs of such a complex group of prisoners.

The solution offered in that earlier chapter was that sufficient volunteers are to be recruited, with sufficient numbers of trained and experienced mentors able to manage the offender population. Not all prisoners would be able to receive an after care service, there are too many prisoners and too few volunteers. Those receiving the service would be restricted to a pre selected group based on local facilities, and expertise. It is recognised this is unsatisfactory, but the only possible solution given the enormity of the problem. Probation Officers would act as mentors if required, but more likely be available to mentor the mentors. Dealing with this group of ex-prisoners involves coping with ethical and moral problems which if not handled appropriately may quickly lead to burnout, resulting in a high turnover of staff with all the attendant problems that creates.

This is not a problem for the Probation Service alone, but for other parts of the criminal justice system. It is a problem for the courts in their sentencing practices, for the prisons in the way they offer rehabilitative programmes, and for the government in the restrictions and barriers it presents to the prisons. (There is no better example than in the way substance misusers are formally prescribed controlled drugs during their sentence making it impossible to be discharged drug free.) To place the onus for success on the Probation Service was unfair, as it was to suggest that reconviction rates were their sole responsibility. There is only so much the Probation Service can do, and it was unrealistic to expect more.

The fourth area of interest is the preparation of reports to the courts. Preparing and submitting reports to the courts have traditionally been an integral part of the Probation Service's work. Rob Canton and Jane Dominey say that the practice of submitting reports to the court can be traced back to the very beginnings of probation where reports read more like a plea.[31] In 2010 over 200,000 were presented. There has been a reduction in the last few years which the Ministry of Justice puts down to "the long term downward trend in the number of cases being dealt with by the Courts."[32]

As things stand reports are prepared by the NPS with assistance from the CRCs who may provide some of the information if they know the offender. It remains to be seen whether this division of responsibility will lead to a disruptive lack of continuity in the supervision process, or will it be resolved in some way. It was not seen as a problem by the local magistrates in Nottingham, who said they were satisfied with the provision and quality of the reports post privatisation. Some said the quality and presentation had actually improved, others that they were no worse than before. Similarly, the Public Accounts Committee said reports to the court also varied in quality, with written reports much better than the reports presented orally. However, some court staff knew little about the work of the CRCs, which could have repercussions later.[33] It is not a satisfactory way of doing things.

The purpose of reports to the courts, often called Pre Sentence Reports or PSRs, is defined by Section 158 of the Criminal Justice Act 2003. A PSR is a report which is completed (a) with a view to assisting the court in determining the most suitable method of dealing with an offender, is made or submitted by an appropriate officer, and (b) contains information as to such matters presented in such manner as may be prescribed by rules made by the Secretary of State. Currently there are three different types of reports submitted or presented to the courts. The most inclusive is the Special Delivery Report, which usually requires a three week adjournment period to complete, and is reserved for high risk offenders. These reports include a thorough risk assessment and a detailed sentencing plan. The Probation Circular (06/2009) entitled "Determining pre sentence reports" referred to this "Standard Delivery Report" which it said should "include consideration of issues where a sentence may have in an adverse effect on the safety of children, of a partner or other identifiable victim."[34] Apparently, standard delivery reports should only be used when it was not possible to use what it called the "Fast Delivery Report," which is a shortened version and is for offenders carrying a medium risk. It requires only a one week adjournment. Finally, there is the Stand Down or Oral Report, which is described as a "verbal report" to be completed on the day of the court and used for medium and low risk cases.[35]

Not only has there been a reduction of Special Delivery Reports but a further reduction (of 63%) of Standard Delivery Reports over the same period, but offset by a commensurate rise in the numbers of Fast Delivery Reports. It is too much of a coincidence to believe there is no connection between privatisation and a reduction in the court's use of reports generally, but as yet there is no evidence to link them directly. There is however a strong suspicion that the increase in the use of Fast Delivery Reports is related to demands of efficiency and follow from government's demands to reduce costs.

The current PSRs have moved a long way from those presented in the 1960s and 1970s. They differ mainly in terms of content and aims. Earlier reports concentrated on the rehabilitation of the offender as well as providing an appropriate recommendation as to the sentence. The current situation is less concerned with rehabilitation, more an adjunct to the sentencing options of the court, a sort of advisory system for the magistracy. The distance travelled has been extensive but has it led to improvements? The answer is equivocal; in some respects yes, in others no.

There are two areas where there has been change for the better. First there are now more restrictions on the courts' use of adjournments. In that earlier period requests for reports invariably involved a lengthy adjournment, often in custody, and often unnecessarily so. The offender spent two weeks or so in custody invariably for a one hour interview by the Probation Officer. It was described thus; "the probation service historically requested that the court adjourned for 3 weeks or more in order that pre sentence advice and information could be assembled and provided".[36] It wasn't quite like that. Often the adjournment was for two not three weeks, and the probation report was often accompanied by a request for a medical report. Nonetheless, the point was made, that a lengthy adjournment was unnecessary, and needlessly expensive, financially or otherwise. No one suggests we return to that. In fact the modern view is that "the new expectations are that most advice to the court can be given on the day the defendant pleads guilty, so as to avoid adjournment and allow for an immediate sentence decision."[37]

Second, there are now more demands for clarity and uniformity concerning the contents of the reports. Earlier reports were idiosyncratic in their content and varied in the way they were presented. (Someone once suggested the only common features were the offender's name and date of birth!) Under that earlier interpretation of what were believed to be the causes of crime and the rehabilitation of the offender, almost anything or everything was relevant. Reports became a highly personalised account derived from the individual Probation Officer's personal view, with little or no attempt to require justification. Standardisation was a necessary and welcome introduction, so that over the years the content of the reports have become tightly prescribed. They now require less information on rehabilitation, more on an analysis of the offence and pattern of offending, together with relevant offender circumstances, showing links either as contributing factors or as protective factors, i.e. providing details linking the offender's background to the crime. These must be set against risk assessments and offence analysis and the impact on the victims. These assessments use RSR Scores (Risk of Serious Recidivism) and OGRS Scores (Offender Group Reconviction Scales), i.e. assessments which help predict reoffending rates. Oral Reports are less concerned with serious harm, but provide an offence analysis on the victim. Templates are provided for each officer.

Critics such as NAPO argue that Same Day Reports (SDRs) and Oral Reports do not allow sufficient time to carry out checks with police and children's services, resulting in these risks going unnoticed. It says these failings lead potentially to inappropriate sentencing and case allocation, but it gives no evidence to support this claim. It also says these failings undermine effective public protection and risk management in the community, but again gives no evidence to support this assertion. Nonetheless, in principle NAPO's claims seems broadly correct. Other critics such as Rob Canton and Jane Dominey are particularly concerned with SDRs, which they say lead to mechanistic responses from offenders, in which officers give superficial accounts of the offence and offer unrealistic commitments for the future.[38]

Canton and Dominey touch on a more important point when they say traditionally PSRs have involved a process of dialogue and negotiation in anticipation of a sentence producing future work.[39] Traditionally, the outcome has been a sentence which involves agreement with Probation Officer, the court, and offender. The current system does not provide that opportunity, especially that involving SDRs. In fact it seems the whole system is no longer concerned to promote principles of rehabilitation, but has become a veiled attempt at promoting utilitarian justice in the form of harm reduction. This involves a radical departure from the traditions of the service, but of course is entirely suited to neo liberalism, especially that form promoted by Carter in the 1990s.

The dangers which come from departing from the traditions of rehabilitation are that the Probation Service becomes an arm of the judiciary, indistinguishable from the magistracy, and there in order to help the court solve problems of sentencing. This is not the direction I think it should go. For all the dangers which came from that earlier form of unbridled rehabilitation, an attachment to a rehabilitative ideal had the merit of offering a distinctive service to the courts and the criminal justice system generally. Accordingly, reports to the courts should reflect this, and not move towards some form of technological wizardry, aimed at solving judicial problems. Lessons can be learned from earlier reflections on report writing, and in this respect there is no better example than that from the Streatfeild Committee in 1961.[40] That committee said reports should contain:

> essential details of the offenders home surroundings and family background: his attitude to his family and their response to him: his school and work record and spare time activities: his attitude to his

> employment: his attitude to the present offence: his attitude and response to previous forms of treatment following previous convictions: detailed histories about relevant physical and mental conditions: an assessment of personality and character.[41]

Stretfeild emphasised important details of the offender's background, together with key figures in the offenders' life, important life events, and circumstances and attitude towards the relevant offence. Taken together, Stretfeild asked for a comprehensive explanation of the crime, in rehabilitative terms that is, where the offence was neither central, nor the determining factor. It suggested reports should embrace a rehabilitative model concerned directly with the offender's motivation, including details of his/her background. All of which helped explain the offence.

That view seems not to be acceptable nowadays. Stretfeild accepted that probation reports should do more than provide information on the offender's background, they should offer an explanation of the offence. This gives a clue to one of the major justifications for court reports generally; they provide an opportunity for offenders to present their side of the story in ways not hitherto available. They should in my view provide more than an account of the offender's personal history, and of a list of individual failings, but give an explanation of criminality in an account not available elsewhere. Of course that information could come from other sources, the police – as it often does – or from psychiatrists where a medical report is required, or perhaps from defence counsel. In which case there would be no need to add or duplicate to what is already there. But these additional sources of information are not always available, nor do they come in that prescribed form.

The current situation requires reports to be brief, providing limited details of the offender. Yet if, as I suggest, the aim is more of a rehabilitative service then a more comprehensive type of report is necessary – more akin to those provided earlier but not so idiosyncratic. That means including more details about the offender than have been required hitherto. Modern reports are less offender centred, and accordingly have lost some of the earlier value. It is unfortunate that the type of information found in the rehabilitative model is no longer required. My suggestion for inclusion in reports are the following.

They would have much of what is currently required, but with more features which allow the offender's account to be included. The template I offer suggest reports should contain the following:

Socio-demographic details. This means basic details such as age, address previous convictions.

Nature of offence. This means the offence and the basic details as provided to the court.

Attitude towards offence. The offender's perception of the offence where it occurred and the circumstances that led up to the offence.

Details of background as they apply to the offence. This is the centre of the report and should contain details of the offender's background and the explanation for this and previous criminality.

Risk assessment including safety of any children or spouse. As currently required.

Victim assessment. The victim's assessment and view of impact of offence, as required

Opinion or recommendation. The suggested sentence.

In this way it would be possible to preserve the continuity of the relationship between the Probation Service and the courts, yet develop and reinforce the bridge between the offender, the demand for rehabilitation and the court's integrity. Above all it would emphasise the importance of rehabilitation as part of the Probation Service's remit.

Traditionally, probation reports have contained an "informed opinion" (sometimes called a "recommendation") which it gives to the court. Often these opinions were accepted implying that the Probation Service has had an important influence of sentencing practices. It was predicted by some commentators that there would be disquiet on the part of sentencers about a private company preparing reports. Courts, it is said, would struggle to take a private company report writer seriously.[42] But this seems not to be so. It is more about the extent of contact between the officers and the courts. Rob Allen and Mike Hough say that research has shown a higher rate of congruity between proposals made by Probation Officers and the sentencing decisions made by a court where the report writer is known to the court.[43] That CRC officers no longer appear in court, nor do they produce reports or are seen by the courts, will mean their impact on sentencing practices will eventually be lost. That may or may not have serious implications. Only time will tell.

3. The ethos of the service

Assume there will be changes after a number of years, then what should those changes be? What would a new look Probation Service look like? Would it involve more privatisation? That is an option albeit an unlikely one, but an option nonetheless. It would mean the CRCs, or a similar set of organisations would take over the whole of the service, including having a role in the courts. It would mean additional areas of practice are outsourced. Given the current interest in the use of the private sector in public service this is a possible alternative. It would relegate the NPS to a subordinate role where it would be working for, not with the CRCs leaving the NPS with a minor part to play. One could see how this would appeal to those intent on promoting that neo liberal ideal.

But there are other options. One that persists in the literature is to return to a form of "Golden Age" type Probation Service. This would be the recreation of a traditional Probation Service, able to service all courts, criminal and otherwise, and remain true to its social work roots. It would return it to the courts and the community, seen as probation's rightful home. This solution would also involve returning to the traditions of the service and revert to the mantra of "advise, assist and befriend," or perhaps "advise, assist, befriend and supervise."

There are still many, including Lord Ramsbotham, who see this as a plausible alternative. His view of the Probation Service fits with the duty of the state "to help those convicted by the Courts to live useful and law abiding lives." The only way to achieve this is a traditional Probation Service which Lord Ransbotham defined in the House of Lords Debate.[44] He said: "At the heart a distinct role of the probation service within the criminal justice system is person-to-person supervision and rehabilitation of offenders awarded community sentences."

It is not easy to see how this could happen. The distance travelled has been too far, and the changes made too extensive to think it possible to return to those earlier roots. Nor would many serving officers, trained under the new rules and regulations, understand why a return was required. It is doubtful if they have an appetite for a system which was part of a bygone era. The Probation Order, once the centre of the Probation Officer's work, has long since vanished, having been merged with a Community Service Order in the 1990s. Traditional methods of working such as home visiting have also been reduced in importance. It would also involve unravelling a complex web of rules, regulations, training packages, and legislation. There is little possibility of that happening.

There are political considerations too. The Probation Service has never been free of political considerations, nor able to remain outside the political debate. When Tony Blair in 1993 said the Labour Government would be "tough on crime, tough on the causes of crime" he was making no less an appeal to a "popular punitive" rhetoric than was Michael Howard some two years later with his insistence that "Prison Works." Both were saying that they saw punishment as being at the heart of criminal justice policy, and that rehabilitation in whatever form, was of secondary importance. It is unlikely therefore that any future government will return to that period where it would accept the luxury of a service which claims it was not punitive. A revamped Probation Service would not be accepted unless it showed that probation works. The Probation Service has to be more than be that "small island of decency and humanity in the criminal justice system." It must show that it is able to reduce offending according to certain precepts and do so at a reduced cost. That puts it within the political debate, and as governments are keen to show their criminological credentials, the most important of which are that it has institutions capable of reducing crime. That means the Probation Service must show it can act on the government's behalf in this respect

Other changes have taken place which make it difficult if not impossible to return to that earlier world. The very concept itself is being challenged as never before. Some critics even suggest that "probation itself is dead," or if not then it remains "a vague and uninspiring term." They say probation as traditionally practiced was "based on the rather bizarre assumption that surveillance with some guidance can steer the offender straight."[45] Or, that reporting to a Probation Officer once every two weeks or so, and/or receiving an occasional home visit, each lasting for about 20 minutes, with the Probation Officer providing insights into the offender's behaviour, cannot expect to reduce criminality. Except of course that for some offenders it did – although apparently not sufficiently often to please recent governments.

Other more extensive changes have occurred which make a return improbable. The so-called neo liberal form of management which demands improved economy, effectiveness, and efficiency is firmly established as government policy. A return to those days where clinicians decided on treatments and governments were expected to pay for them seem unlikely. "Advise assist and befriend" was, according to one Probation Officer currently working for a CRC, "too centred on the assessment of individual officers." He was more enthusiastic about the current approach which is based more on IT use, and where costs are built into assessments.

The future of the Probation Service must also be seen within the context of current conditions, financial or otherwise. The Probation Service remains a comparatively small service when set against the police or prison system, and will, in spite of claims that its voice should be heard, remain that way unless its governance alters. Many of its traditional claims will not resonate with governments. It may say that offenders have a right to be heard and the criminal justice system should represent their views, but this remains a minority view. And anyway, Maurice Vanstone reminds us it does not have a monopoly of fairness and social justice, even if it does have a history of providing the criminal justice system with a perspective about offending based on those values.[46] Set against other government demands such as those of social care, it is unlikely the Probation Service could expect to be given priority. There are more pressing problems, financial and otherwise, for governments to deal with.

The wish to return to a more traditional stance is provided somewhat whimsically by Peter Raynor, who says one idea that often appeals is to start again. He wants to persuade a group of magistrates to accept the attachment of a voluntary social worker to their court; perhaps somebody from a faith backed group to talk to offenders, to help those who needed or wanted help to stay out of trouble. Perhaps not so whimsical after all, but hardly likely to happen.[47]

Returning to that earlier world where Probation Officers were seen, and saw themselves, as independent providers of rehabilitation, or rather providing their own distinct form, is against wider social trends. As Britain moves increasingly towards a meritocratic view there is less sympathy with those who fail. A culture which supports equality of opportunity takes a harsher view of those who cannot meet its demands. In contrast a culture which provides a more enclosed system of class, will appear more sympathetic to those who fall outside its boundaries.[48] Returning to a more class ridden view is again unlikely.

Privatisation is not without its supporters, and some see merit in many if not all the current changes. They want to keep some and remove others. They believe it might be possible to envisage ways of working that integrate the best of traditions of probation drawing on the resources of the private sector. They may not seek a Level 1 type privatisation programme but might accept something akin to Levels 2 and 3. Their dystopian view is of an increasingly fragmented model of service delivery controlled by a small number of multinational companies, and mainly driven by the imperatives of cost reduction and profit maximisation. Their utopian view is a mixture of public and private sectors working in harmony.

Keeping some aspects of privatisation and rejecting others is one way forward. The debate will of course always be about which features to keep and which to jettison. A favoured theme is that probation needed to change, that the private sector should be encouraged to be involved as it brings in new ideas, but the public sector should be there to provide that bulwark against reductions in responsibility and accountability. The private sector must meet these requirements if its place is to be secured. But there are always likely to be tensions wherever public and private sectors work together. Lol Burke puts it this way:

> There are also obvious issues of legitimacy and accountability when statutory responsibilities are given to profit making organisations whose lines of accountability to the court and public are less clear. In a chain of contracts involving a complex web of providers and service delivery arrangements it becomes more difficult to establish responsibility when they go wrong.[49]

And things will go wrong, and when they do apportioning blame will be difficult. Those having the most to lose are likely to react the most strongly, as would be expected when disputes occur between parties with separate aims and objectives. In the case of the privatised Probation Service tensions are likely to occur where CRCs have a financial interest. It is interesting that, in spite of the many changes and the threat to the service basic assumptions on which the Probation Service was born will remain. They may not be based on the old model of "advise, assist and befriend" but they stay remarkably close to it, and unfashionable it may be to say it, the Probation Service may have benefitted from the changes and upheavals experienced these past years. The return to an integrated public service as of old may not be possible, but one where the public and private sectors work together may well be feasible. As I keep saying preparation for that future is the key, and clarity of purpose the aim. It will all depend on how much we want it.

What sort of service do we want? I suggest here that its governance will be such as to provide more direct contact with government giving it more influence and thereby more protection. I suggest too that it will be required to supervise offenders in the community, and that supervision will be more responsive to the needs of the offenders without losing the importance of being able to enforce rules and regulations built into that supervision. Finally, I suggest the ethos of the service will involve a mixture of the public and private, this being the only way to prevent the service from being overwhelmed by one rather than the other.

I have tried to answer some of the questions posed by Dame Glenys Stacey when she asks "What sort of Probation Service do we want," if that is, we want one at all? The solutions offered are based on a mixture of present and past events which involve an implicit belief in the value of a service able to offer something distinct in criminal justice. The form of privatisation offered in 2014 might not be the way forward, but some of the principles of the private sector are to be welcomed. Marrying these with some of the traditions of the past would seem to offer a better way forward.

If Barbara Wootton was correct and that crime rates rise and fall irrespective of the actions of the criminal justice system and irrespective of changes in government policy, then the role of prisons is simply to contain, and that of the courts to dispense justice. On the face of it that leaves the Probation Service in a rather anomalous position, losing its role as a rehabilitative agency, and leaving open questions about its impact on desistance from crime. Except that there are other offerings to be made which are equally valuable, if not more so. These are less tangible but no less important and based on the impact a Probation Service could have on society's wellbeing. The most important is to emphasise that individuals can change their behaviour, often with encouragement and assistance, and a Probation Service is ideally placed to promote that view. The Probation Service then becomes an institutionalised expression of certain values that people can change, and as such offers hope rather than propagate a more dogmatic pessimism that human behaviour is fixed, and criminal behaviour firmly fixed.

More than this, such a value system suggests human society is safer when we include rather than exclude offenders. Outcasts can sometimes be dangerous and violent criminal outcasts particularly so. Better to have them within rather than without. Outcasts of course come in many different forms, the outcasts from some of our housing estates are no less outcasts than the mentally disordered offender who randomly and violently seeks victims. And it is no less a challenge to bring the former into the mainstream of society than the latter. Some young men (they are invariably young men) show a palpable failure to be part of mainstream society. That failure was evident at an early age, with poor educational attainment and an equal failure in the employment market, both of which sets them apart from their more integrated colleagues, but not necessarily sets them apart from others in the same housing estate. The result can be large numbers of similar young men, all in their way outcasts with few opportunities and even fewer prospects. That about one third of short term prisoners go from one prison sentence to another, from one relationship to another, and from one set of drug rituals to another, is the nature of the problem. Breaking that circle of failure is never going to be an easy task.

We may not always succeed, failures are to be expected, but that is not an excuse for not trying. Expecting and working for change in behaviour from those who regularly appear before the courts, those that Robert Reiner describes as "police property," presents the most daunting task. Changes in behaviour are more likely to be achieved by changes in circumstances, a job, with some prospects, and a stability of relationships, but these are rarely forthcoming. More is needed; there has to be a support system that extends to the immediate family, and almost certainly there needs to be someone who offers hope for the future, and that almost certainly means a Probation Officer. In David Faulkner's terms, the Probation Service must be outward looking with the skills of listening and consultation, and the ability to manage conflicts, tensions and ambiguities.[50] It puts the Probation Service in a role of promoting citizenship where offenders and their families are people "in the same spirit."

This role would not fit easily with the traditional Probation Service of the late 20th Century, but could do so nowadays – and this in spite of recent changes. The service is more inclined to be outward looking and have a greater influence in local communities than before. It is more willing to promote projects that have a practical effect. It can be more than "modest but useful," as it was once described, in that it can offer strategies which help include those who are excluded, and give hope to those whose experiences suggest otherwise. It would still need to be controlled by government and deliver according to the Home Office's aims of "the effective execution of sentences of the courts so as to reduce reoffending and protect the public," but in doing so can offer much that is unique.

Notes

1 HM Inspectorate of Probation for England and Wales (2015) Annual Report 2015. Pg. 12.
2 HM Inspectorate of Probation for England and Wales (2017) Annual Report 2017. See also Ministry of Justice (2018) *Strengthening probation, building confidence*, Cm 9613.
3 Lord Ramsbotham. Pers. Com.
4 Ministry of Justice (2018) op. cit. Para 16.
5 Stacey G (2017) Next steps in probation reform in England and Wales. Speech to the Westminster Legal Policy Forum (7th November).
6 HM Inspectorate of Probation for England and Wales (2017) Quality and impact inspection. The effectiveness of probation work in Cumbria. (5th October). See also HM Inspectorate of Probation for England and Wales (2018) The effectiveness of probation work by the National Probation Service in London. (10th January), and House of Commons Justice Committee (2018) Transforming Rehabilitation. HC 482. (30th January 2018).

7 Stacey G (2017) Probation services – getting back on track. Portal Lecture. Institute of Probation. Sheffield. (13th June).
8 Stacey G (2017) Can probation services deliver what we want and expect? Speech to the Criminal Justice Management Conference. (19th September).
9 National Audit Office Report (2017) An investigation into changes to Community Rehabilitation Company contracts. (19th December). In the first quarter of 2017 the volume of activity was between 16% and 48% less than originally anticipated, with the numbers supervised by CRCs up by 20%. This led to a reduction in the expected amount to be paid for the duration of the contracts from £3.7b to £2.1b. Projected losses are of £443m from 2016 to 2022 if contracts are not amended.
10 Lord Woolf. (1991) *The Woolf Report. A summary of the main findings and 22 recommendations of the inquiry into prison disturbances.*
11 Home Office (1991) Custody, care and justice: the way ahead for the prison service in England and Wales. HMSO.
12 Lord Ramsbotham. Pers Com.
13 House of Commons Justice Committee (2018) Oral Evidence on Transforming Rehabilitation. HC 482. (30 January). Q 186.
14 National Probation Service for England and Wales (2001) A new choreography: an integrated strategy for the National Probation Service for England and Wales. HMSO.
15 NAPO (2011) Briefing paper. National Standards.
16 Leibling A (2006) Lessons from prison privatisation for probation. In Hough M, Allen R, and Padel U (eds) *Reshaping probation and prisons.* Policy Press. pp. 68–77.
17 Raynor P and Vansytone M Letter to the Guardian. 1st April 2015.
18 HM Inspectorate of Probation for England and Wales (2017) op. cit. Pg. 6.
19 Parole supervision requires a high level of professionalism involving complex levels of enforcement. This can only come after extensive periods of training. It is clearly more complex than other forms of supervision as it invariably involves more serious offenders.
20 Ministry of Justice (2015) National Standards for the Management of Offenders in England and Wales. (1st Feb).
21 Bottoms A (2001) Compliance and community penalties. In Bottoms A, Gelsthorpe L, and Rex S (eds) *Community penalties: changes and challenges.* Willan Publishing. pp. 87–116.
22 Faulkner D. Pers. Com.
23 Webster R (19th October 2017) Why are offenders recalled to prison? Online at russellwebster.com.
24 Maguire M and Raynor P (2006) How the resettlement of prisoners promotes desistance from crime. Or does it? *Criminology and Criminal Justice.* Vol. 6, No. 1, pp. 19–38. Pg. 33., and Prison Reform Trust (2017) *Prisons. The facts.*
25 Faulkner D. Pers. Com.
26 Hearnden I and Millie A (2004) Does tougher enforcement lead to lower reconvictions? *Probation Journal.* Vol. 51, No. 1, pp 48–58.

27 Mair G and Canton R (2007) Sentencing, community penalties and the role of the probation service. In Gelsthorpe L and Morgan R (eds) *Handbook of probation*. Willan Publishing. pp. 248–291. Pg. 270.
28 Bottoms A (2001) op. cit. Pg. 103.
29 Ibid. Pg. 101.
30 HM Inspectorate of Probation for England and Wales (2016) An inspection of Through The Gate resettlement services for discharged prisoners serving 12 months or more. (October). Pg. 7.
31 Canton R and Dominey J (2018) *Probation* (Second Edition). Routledge. Pg. 86.
32 Ministry of Justice (2017) Offender management systems bulletin. *England and Wales Quarterly*. (April to June). Pg. 9.
33 House of Commons Public Accounts Committee (2016) Report. Transforming Rehabilitation. HC 484. (September). Paras 10 and 12.
34 National Offender Management Service (NOMS) and Ministry of Justice (2017). Determining pre sentence report and sentencing within the new framework. (March).
35 NOMS (2003) Determining pre sentence reports, and Ministry of Justice (2011) Determining pre sentence reports.
36 HM Inspectorate of Probation for England and Wales (2017) *The work of the Probation Service in courts*. (June). Pg. 6.
37 Ibid. Pg. 6.
38 Canton R and Dominey J (2018) op. cit. Pg. 39.
39 Ibid. Pg. 93.
40 HMSO (1961) *Interdepartmental committee on the business of the Criminal Courts* (The Stretfeild Committee Report).
41 Ibid. Pg. 95.
42 Allen R and Hough M (2007) Community penalties, sentencers, the media and the public opinion. In Gelsthorpe L and Morgan R (eds) *Handbook of probation*. Willan Publishing. pp. 565–590. Pg. 586.
43 Ibid. Pg. 586.
44 House of Lords Debates (2010) Hansard, Cm 1143. (21 December).
45 Meloney D, Brazemore G, and Hudson J (2001) The end of probation and the beginning of community justice. *Perspectives*. Vol. 25, pp. 22–30. Pg. 22–30 and 272. See also Nellis M and Chui W (eds) *Moving probation forward*. Pearson Longman
46 Vanstone M (2004) *Supervising offenders in the community*. Ashgate. Pg. 159.
47 Raynor P (2012) Is probation still possible? *Howard Journal of Criminal Justice*. Vol. 51, No. 2, pp. 173–206.
48 A slightly different view is from Collett S (2013) Riots, revolution and rehabilitation: the future of probation. *Howard Journal of Criminal Justice*. Vol. 52, No. 2, pp. 163–189.
49 Editorial (2013) Grayling's hubris. *Probation Journal*. Vol. 60, No. 4, pp. 377–382. Pg. 379.
50 Faulkner D (2002) Probation, citizenship and public service. In Ward D, Scott J, and Lacey M (eds) *Probation: working for justice*. Oxford University Press. pp. 39–52.

APPENDICES

APPENDIX 1: PRIME MINISTERS FROM 1990 TO 2018

John Major: 28th November 1990–2nd May 1997
Tony Blair: 2nd May 1997–27th June 2007
Gordon Brown: 27th June 2007–11th May 2010
David Cameron/Nick Clegg: 11th May 2010–8th May 2015
David Cameron: 8th May 2015–13th July 2016
Theresa May: 13th July 2016–

APPENDIX 2: HOME SECRETARIES FROM NOVEMBER 1990 TO JULY 2016

Kenneth Baker: 28th November 1990–10th April 1992
Kenneth Clarke: 10th April 1992–27th May 1993
Michael Howard: 27th May 1993–2nd May 1997
Jack Straw: 2nd May 1997–8th June 2001
David Blunkett: 8th June 2001–15th December 2004
Charles Clarke: 15th December 2004–5th May 2006
John Reid: 5th May 2006–27th June 2007
Jacquie Smith: 27th June 2007–5th June 2009
Alan Johnson: 5th June 2009–11th May 2010
Theresa May: 11th May 2010–13th July 2016

The Ministry of Justice took over some Home Office duties in May 2007. Kenneth Clarke was Secretary of State and Lord Chancellor from May 2010 until September 2012, followed by Chris Grayling from September 2012 until May 2015.

BIBLIOGRAPHY

Allen R and Hough M (2006) Endnote. In Hough M, Allen R, and Padel U (eds) *Reshaping probation and prisons*. Policy Press. pp. 95–102.

Allen R and Hough M (2007) Community penalties, sentencers, the media and public opinion. In Gelsthorpe L and Morgan R (eds) *Handbook of probation*. Willan Publishing. pp. 565–590.

Audit Commission (2012) *Right data: right payment*. Audit Commission.

Audit Commission (2012a) *By definition: improving data definitions and their use by the NHS; a briefing from the Payment by Results data assurance programme*. Audit Commission.

Bean P T (1976) *Rehabilitation and deviance*. Routledge.

Bean P T (2014) *Drugs and crime* (4th Edition). Routledge.

Bean P T and Nemitz T (1995) Discrepancies and inaccuracies in statistics for detained patients. *Psychiatric Bulletin*. Vol. 19, No. 1, pp. 28–32.

Bennett A (2014) Foreward. In Statham R (ed) *The golden age of probation*. Waterside Press. p. vii.

Bottoms A (2001) Compliance and community penalties. In Bottoms A, Gelsthorpe L and Rex S (2001) (eds) *Community penalties: change and challenges*. Willan Publishing. pp. 87–116.

Bottoms A and McWilliams B (1979) A non-treatment paradigm for probation practice. *British Journal of Social Work*. Vol. 9, No. 2, pp. 159–202.

Bottoms A, Rex S and Robertson G (2004) (eds) *Alternatives to prison*. Willan Publishing.

Burke L and Collett S (2010) People are not things; what New Labour has done to probation. *Probation Journal*. Vol. 57, No. 3, pp. 232–249.

Burke L and Collett S (2015) *Delivering rehabilitation: the politics governance and control of probation*. Routledge.

Burke L and Collett S (2016) Transforming probation; organizational bifurcation and the end of probation as we know it. *Probation Journal*. Vol. 63, No. 2, pp. 120–135.

Burnett R, Baker K and Roberts C (2007) Assessment, supervision and intervention; fundamental practice in probation. In Gelsthorpe L and Morgan R (eds) *Handbook of probation*. Willan Publishing. pp. 210–247.

Cannings J (2014) A view of probation in the 1960s; from the bottom. In Statham R (ed) *The golden age of probation*. Waterside Press. pp. 97–106.

Canton R and Dominey J (2018) *Probation* (2nd Edition). Routledge.

Carr N (2017) Goodbye NOMS – Where to next? *Probation Journal*. Vol. 64, No. 2, pp. 91–93.

Carter E and Whitwell A (2015) Creaming and parking in quasi-marketed welfare at work schemes. *Journal of Social Policy*. Vol. 44, No. 2, pp. 277–296.

Carter P (2003) *Managing offenders reducing crime: the correctional services review*. The Strategy Unit.

Carter P (2007) *Securing the future: proposals for the efficient and sustainable use of custody in England and Wales*. Cabinet Office.

Chui W (2003) What works in reducing offending: principles and programmes. In Chui W H and Nellis M (eds) *Moving probation forward*. Pearson Longman. pp. 56–73.

Chui W and Nellis M (2003) (eds) *Moving probation forward*. Pearson Longman.

Chui W and Nellis M (2003) Creating the National Probation Service – New wine in old bottles. In Chui W and Nellis M (eds) *Moving probation forward*. Pearson Longman. pp. 1–18.

Clare R (2015) Maintaining professional practice: the role of the probation officer in community rehabilitation companies. *Probation Journal*. Vol. 62, No. 1, pp. 49–61.

Collett S (2013) Riots, revolution and rehabilitation: the future of probation. *Howard Journal of Criminal Justice*. Vol. 52, No. 2, pp. 163–189.

Conservative Party (2009) *Prisons with a purpose: our sentencing and rehabilitation revolution to break the cycle of crime*. The Conservative Party.

Courier Mail(2018) 1 January.

Day M (1987) The politics of probation. In Harding J (ed) *Probation and the community*. Tavistock. pp. 21–34.

Deering J and Feilzer M (2015) *Privatising probation*. Policy Press.

Department of Health (2012) *A simple guide to payment by results*. (Ref. 18135).

Dominey J (2012) A mixed market for probation services: can lessons from the recent past help shape the Future? *Probation Journal*. Vol. 59, No. 4, pp. 339–354.

Editorial. (2013) Grayling's hubris. *Probation Journal*. Vol. 60, No. 4, pp. 377–382.

Editorial. (2014) The Probation Institute: more than an after thought? *Probation Journal*. Vol. 61, No. 1, pp. 3–7.

Faulkner D (2002) Probation, citizenship and public service. In Ward D, Scott J and Lacey M (eds) *Probation: working for justice*. Oxford University Press. pp. 39–52.

Faulkner D (2006) A modern service, fit for purpose? In Hough M, Allen R, and Padel U (eds) *Reshaping probation and prisons*. Policy Press. pp. 79–93.

Financial Times (2018) UK Finance watchdog exposes lost PFI millions. (17th January).

Fitzgibbon W (2013) Risk and rrivatisation. *British Journal of Community Justice*. Vol. 11, Nos. 2–3, pp. 87–90.

Fitzgibbon W and Lea J (2014) Defending probation; beyond privatisation and security. *European Journal of Probation*. Vol. 6, No. 1, pp. 24–41.

Fox C and Albertson K (2012) Is Payment by Results the most efficient way to address the challenges faced by the criminal justice sector? *Probation Journal*. Vol. 59, No. 4, pp. 355–373.

Fullwood C (2002) The social and Criminal Policy context. In Ward D, Scott J and Lacey M (eds) *Probation: working for justice*. Oxford University Press. pp. 53–63.

Gelsthorpe L and Morgan R (2007) (eds) *Handbook of probation*. Willan Publishing.

Genders E (2002) Legitimacy, accountability and private prisons. *Punishment and Society*. Vol. 4, No. 3, pp. 285–303.

Hall S (2015) Why probation matters. *Howard Journal of Criminal Justice*. Vol. 54, No. 4, pp. 321–335.

Harding J (1999) The probation service in the 20th century. *Criminal Justice Matters*. No. 38, pp. 27–28.

Hearnden I and Millie A (2004) Does tougher enforcement lead to lower reconvictions? *Probation Journal*. Vol. 51, No. 1, pp. 48–58.

Hedderman C (2013) Payment by results: hopes and fears. *British Journal of Community Justice*. Vol. 11, Nos. 2–3, pp. 43–58.

Hedderman C and Hough M (2004) Getting tough or being effective: what matters? In Mair G (ed) *What matters in probation*. Willan Publishing. pp. 146–169.

HM Inspectorate of Probation and HM Inspectorate of Prisons (2016) An inspection of Through The Gate services for short term prisoners. A Joint Inspection by HM Inspectorate of Probation and HM Inspectorate of Prisons (October).

HM Inspectorate of Probation for England and Wales (2015) Annual Report 2015.

HM Inspectorate of Probation for England and Wales (2016) An inspection of Through The Gate resettlement services for short term prisoners.

HM Inspectorate of Probation for England and Wales (2017) The work of the Probation Services in courts. (June).

HM Inspectorate of Probation for England and Wales (2017) The implementation and delivery of rehabilitation activity requirements.

HM Inspectorate of Probation for England and Wales (2017) Quality and impact inspection. The effectiveness of Probation Work in West Mercia.

HM Inspectorate of Probation for England and Wales (2017) Quality and impact inspection. The effectiveness of Probation Work in Cumbria. (5th October).

HM Inspectorate of Probation for England and Wales (2017) Annual Report 2017.

HM Inspectorate of Probation for England and Wales (2017) An inspection of Through The Gate resettlement services for discharged prisoners serving 12 months or more. (October).

HM Inspectorate of Probation in England and Wales (2018) The effectiveness of probation work by the National Probation Service in London. (10th January).

HM Inspectorate of Probation in England and Wales (2018) Enforcement and Recall. (February).

HM Prison and HM Probation Services for England and Wales (2017) Joint Report. (5th April).

HMSO (1961) Interdepartmental committee on the business of the Criminal Courts (The Stretfeild Committee Report).

Home Office (1962) Report of the Departmental Committee of the Probation Service (The Morison Report). HMSO.

Home Office (1984) Statement of National Objectives and Priorities. (SNOP).

Home Office (1991) Custody, care and justice: the way ahead for the prison service in England and Wales. HMSO.

Home Office (1995) Strengthening punishment in the Community a consultation document. (March) Cm 2780.

Home Office (1995) National Standards for the Supervision of Offenders.

Home Office (1998) Joining forces to protect the public: prisons-probation. A consultation Document. Stationery Office.

Home Office (2006) A five year strategy for protecting the public and reducing crime. (Cm 6717).

Hood R and Sparks R (1971) *Key issues in criminology*. Weidenfeld and Nicolson.

Hough M (2006) Introduction. In Hough M, Allen R, and Padel U (eds) *Reshaping probation and prisons*. Policy Press, pp. 1–7.

Hough M, Allen R, and Padel U (2006) (eds) *Reshaping probation and prisons*. Policy Press.

House of Commons (2011) The role of the probation service. *8th Report of Session 2010–2012 HC 519–511*. (27 July 2011).

House of Commons (2014) Crime reduction policies: a coordinated approach? Interim report of the government's Transforming Rehabilitation programme. HC 1004. (January).

House of Commons Justice Committee (2014) Report on Transforming Rehabilitation programme. HC 1004.

House of Commons Justice Committee (2018) Oral Evidence on Transforming Rehabilitation. HC 482. Q 93–128(25). (30th January and 27th February).

House of Commons National Audit Office (2009) National Offender Management Information System. The Stationery Office. (June).

House of Commons Public Accounts Committee (2016) Transforming Rehabilitation inquiry. (June).

House of Commons Public Accounts Committee (2016) Report. Transforming Rehabilitation. HC 484. (September).

House of Commons Public Accounts Committee (2018) Investigation into changes to community rehabilitation companies contracts. HC 897. (March).

Labour Party (1997) Manifesto. Britain will be better with New Labour. Labour Party.

Lacey M (2014) The hat on the door. In Statham R (ed) *The golden age of probation*. Waterside Press. pp.124–147.

Leibling A (2006) Lessons from prison privatisation for probation. In Hough M, Allen R, and Padel U (eds) *Reshaping probation and prisons*. Policy Press, pp. 69–77.

Le Vay J (2016) *Competition for prisons: public or private*. Policy Press.

Lockart-Miriams G, Pickles C, and Crowhurst E (2015) *Cutting crime: the role of tagging in offender management*. Reform Research Trust.

Lord Woolf (1991) The Woolf Report. A summary of the main findings and 22 recommendations of the inquiry into prison disturbances.

Ludlow A (2014) Transforming rehabilitation: what lessons might be learned from prison privatisation? *European Journal of Probation*. Vol. 6, No. 1, pp 67–68.

Maguire M (2007) The resettlement of ex prisoners. In Gelsthorpe L and Morgan R (eds) *Handbook of probation*. Willan Publishing. pp. 398–424.

Maguire M and Raynor P (2006) How the resettlement of prisoners promotes desistance from crime. Or does it? *Criminology and Criminal Justice*. Vol. 6, No. 1, pp. 19–38.

Mair G (2004) The origin of "What Works" in England and Wales: a house built on sand. In Mair G (ed) *What matters in probation*. Willan Publishing. pp. 12–33.

Mair G (2004) (ed) *What matters in probation*. Willan Publishing.

Mair G (2011) The Community order in England and Wales; policy and practice. *Probation Journal*. Vol. 58, No. 3, pp. 215–232.

Mair G (2016) 'A difficult trip I think.' The end days of the probation service in England and Wales? *European Journal of Probation*. Vol. 8, No. 1, pp. 3–15.

Mair G and Burke L (2012) *Redemption, rehabilitation and risk management: a history of probation*. Routledge.

Mair G and Canton R (2007) Sentencing, community penalties and the role of the probation service. In Gelsthorpe L and Morgan R (eds) *Handbook of probation*. Willan Publishing. pp. 248–291.

Mantle G (2006) Probation: dead, dying or poorly? *Howard Journal of Criminal Justice*. Vol. 45, No. 3, pp. 321–324.

Martinson R (1974) What works? Questions and answers about prison reform. *The Public Interest*. Vol. 35, No. 5, pp. 22–54.

Meloney D, Brazemore G, and Hudson J (2001) The end of probation and the beginning of community justice. *Perspectives*. Vol. 25, pp. 22–30.

Ministry of Justice (2010) Breaking the cycle: effective punishment, rehabilitation and sentencing of offenders. (Cm7972) (Dec).

Ministry of Justice (2011) Determining pre sentencing reports.

Ministry of Justice (2011) Payment by Results (October).

Ministry of Justice (2011) Probation service wins excellence award (October).

Ministry of Justice (2012) Punishment and reform: effective probation services. (CP 7/2012) (March).

Ministry of Justice (2012) Punishment and reform: effective community sentences. (CP (R) 7/2012).

Ministry of Justice (2013) Transforming Rehabilitation: a revolution in the way we manage offenders. A strategy for reform. (Cm 8517).

Ministry of Justice (2013) Transforming offenders: a strategy for reform. Response to Consultation (CP 9R. 16/2013). (Cm 8619).

Ministry of Justice (2013) Impact assessment of the Offender Management Bill (May).

Ministry of Justice (2013) Punishment and reform: Summary of Responses (May).

Ministry of Justice (2013) Transforming Rehabilitation: Summary of Responses (May).

Ministry of Justice (2014) Procurement. Transforming Rehabilitation programme. Payment mechanism.

Ministry of Justice (2016) National Standards for the Management of Offenders in England and Wales. (1st February).

Ministry of Justice (2016) Transforming Rehabilitation: The National Audit Office Report. (HC 951).

Ministry of Justice (2017) Offender management systems bulletin. *England and Wales. Quarterly.* (April to June).

Ministry of Justice (2018) Impact Assessment of the Offender Management Bill.

Ministry of Justice (2018) *Strengthening probation, building confidence*. (Cm 9613).

Morgan R (2003) Thinking about the demand for probation services. *Probation Journal*. Vol. 50, No. 1, pp. 7–19.

Morgan R (2007) Probation, governance and accountability. In Gelsthorpe L and Morgan R (eds) *Handbook of probation*. Willan Publishing. pp. 90–113.

National Audit Office (2009) National Offender Management Information System. The Stationary Office.

National Audit Office (2012) Audit Commission Report. Right data. Right Payment. The Stationery Office.

National Audit Office (2012) Audit Commission Report. By definition: improving data definitions and their use by the NHS. The Stationery Office.

National Audit Office (2015) Outcome based payment schemes: government's use of Payment by Results. (HC 86) (June) The Stationery Office.

National Audit Office (2016) Report by the Controller and Auditor: General Transforming Rehabilitation. (April) HC 951.

National Audit Office (2017) An investigation into changes to Community Rehabilitation Company contracts. (December).

National Association of Probation Officers (NAPO) (2011) Briefing paper. Resistance to cuts and privatisation.

National Association of Probation Officers (NAPO) (2011) Briefing paper. Privatisation and the Probation Service.

National Association of Probation Officers (NAPO) (2011) Briefing paper. National Standards.

National Association of Probation Officers (NAPO) (2012) Briefing paper. Probation, privatisation and accountability.

National Association of Probation Officers (NAPO) (2014) Briefing paper. Transforming Rehabilitation on crime reduction, reoffending and probation resources.

National Offender Management Service and Ministry of Justice(NOMS) (2003) Determining pre sentence reports.

National Offender Management Service(NOMS)and Ministry of Justice (2017) Determining pre sentence reports, and sentencing within the new framework. (March).

National Probation Service for England and Wales (2001) A new choreography: an integrated strategy for the National Probation Service in England and Wales. HMSO.

Nellis M (1991) Criminology, crime prevention and the future of probation training. In Bottomley K, Fowles T, and Renier R (eds) *Criminal justice theory and practice*. British Society of Criminology Conference 1991. Selected Papers Vol. 2.

Nellis M (1995) Probation values for the 1990s. *Howard Journal of Criminal Justice*. Vol. 34, No. 1, pp. 19–44.

Nellis M (2003) Electronic Monitoring and the future of Probation. In Chui W and Nellis M (eds) *Moving probation forward*. Pearson Longman. pp. 245–260.

Nellis M (2004) Electronic Monitoring and the community supervision of offenders. In Bottoms A, Rex S and Robinson G (eds) *Alternatives to prison*. Willan Publishing. pp. 224–247.

Nellis M (2006) NOMS, contestability and the process of technocorrectional innovation. In Hough M, Allen R, and Padel U (eds) *Reshaping probation and prisons*. Policy Press. pp. 49–68.

Nellis M and Chui W (2003) The end of probation? In Nellis M and Chui W (eds) *Moving probation forward*. Pearson Longman. pp. 261–275.

Nellis M and Gelsthorpe L (2003) Human rights and the probation values debate. In Chui W and Nellis M (eds) *Moving probation forward*. Pearson Longman. pp. 227–244.

Office for Victims (1999) Promising victim-related practitioners and strategies in probation and parole. US Department of Justice.

Prison Reform Trust (2011) Prison Factfile.

Prison Reform Trust (2017) Prisons. The facts.

Private Eye (11–24 August 2017) *World takes break*. No. 1450.

Raynor P (2012) Is probation still possible? *Howard Journal of Criminal Justice*. Vol. 51, No. 2, pp. 173–206.

Rumgay J (2003) Partnerships in the probation service. In Chui W and Nellis M (eds) *Moving probation forward*. Pearson Longman. pp. 195–213.

Rumgay J (2004) The barking dog? Partnerships and effective practice. In Mair G (ed) *What matters in probation*. Willan Publishing. pp. 122–145.

Stacey C (2012) The marketization of the Criminal Justice System: who is the customer? *Probation Journal*. Vol. 59, No. 4, pp. 406–414.

Stacey G (2016) Submission to the Public Accounts Committee. Transforming Rehabilitation Inquiry. (27th June 2016).

Stacey G (2016) Evidence to the House of Commons, Public Accounts Committee on Transforming Rehabilitation.

Stacey G (2017). Next steps in probation reform in England and Wales. Speech to the Westminster Legal Policy Forum. (7th November 2017).

Stacey G (2017) Probation services: getting back on track. Portal Lecture. Institute of Probation 2nd Annual Conference. Sheffield. (June).

Stacey G (2017) Keynote speech. Clinks Annual Conference. (2nd November).

Stacey G (2017) Can probation services deliver what we want and expect? Speech to the Criminal Justice Management Conference. (19th September).

Statham R (2014) (ed) *The golden age of probation*. Waterside Press.

Taylor S, Burke L, Millings M and Ragonese E (2017) Transforming Rehabilitation during a penal crisis: a case study of Through The Gate services in a resettlement prison in England and Wales. *European Journal of Probation*. Vol. 9, No. 2, pp. 115–131.

Travis A (4th July 2013) Grayling's prisons plan to ensure inmates are released close to home. *The Guardian*.
Treadwell J (2006) Some personal reflections on probation training. *Howard Journal of Criminal Justice*. Vol. 45, No. 1, pp. 1–13.
UK Government (19th July 2017) Probation reform: open letter from the Secretary of State for Justice David Lidington.
Vanstone M (2004) *Supervising offenders in the community*. Ashgate.
Walker H and Beaumont W (1981) *Probation work: critical theory and socialist practice*. Blackwell.
Ward D, Scott J and Lacey M (2002) (eds) *Probation. Working for justice*. Oxford University Press.
Webster R (19th October 2017) Why are offenders recalled to prison? Online at russellwebster.com.
Whitehead P (2010) *Exploring modern probation*. Policy Press.
Williams B and Goodman H (2007) Working for and with the victims of crime. In Gelsthorpe L and Morgan R (eds) *Handbook of probation*. Willan Publishing. pp. 518–541.
Worrall A (2002) Missed opportunities? The probation service and women offenders. In Ward D, Scott J and Lacey M (eds) *Probation: working for justice*. Oxford University Press. pp. 134–148.
Wootton B (1969) *Social science and social pathology*. Allen and Unwin.
Wootton B (1973) Community service. *Criminal Law Review*. (Jan) pp. 16–22.
Wootton B (1977) Some reflections on the first five years of community service. *Probation Journal*. Vol. 24, No. 4, pp. 110–112.

INDEX

advise, assist and befriend 27, 31–32, 32, 33, 160
after care, prison 129–130; *see also* Through The Gate
attribution of success, in PbR 114–115
Association of Chief Officers of Probation (ACOP) 35, 69, 80–81
Audit Office *see* National Audit Office
Augustus, John 7

bidding, by private companies 57, 102–103; *see also* contracts
binary calculations in PbR 110–111, 115
Blair T 89, 171
Budd J and Knivett A 70, 73–74

Carter Patrick (later Lord) 25, 36–53, 68
caseloads, of Probation Service 4, 37, 62, 99
Certificate in Social Work 72
Children and Young Persons Act 1969, 25

Children Family Court Advisory and Support Services (CAFCASS) 45
Clarke, Ken 19, 54, 108
Coalition Government 14
Community Orders 4, 7 28–29, 32, 159, 171
Community Rehabilitation Companies (CRCs) 3, 55; passim, 89; passim, career patterns of CRC officers 97–98; creation of 57–58; governance of CRCs 148–154; staffing of 119–120
community prisons 130
Community Service Order 28–30, 62, 67; *see also* Probation Order
consent requirements in probation 40
Conservative Government 46
contracts of CRCs 101, 102, 117, 121, 145
cost of privatisation 56, 59–60, 88–89, 117, 119, 121
cost of probation service 30, 37
Council of Europe 129

Criminal Justice Act (1948) 2
Criminal Justice Act (1991) 25, 30, 32–33 36

desistance from crime 111, 158
drug courts in USA 162
Drug Treatment and Testing Order 46

effectiveness of probation 28
Electronic Monitoring 33–36, 80–81
Entrants, to the probation service 73–74
ethos of probation 170–176
European Convention on Human Rights 80

Faulkner, David 14, 158, 160
fee for service, in PbR 110–111
fee for use, in PbR 109, 116
frequency metric, in PbR 111

Golden Age of Probation 2, 5, 6, 7, 22, 24, 25–27, 160, 170,
Grayling, Chris 13–14, 52; passim 57, 87, 91, 94, 95, 108 119, 127, 130 136, 138, 144
Governance, of the probation service 68–69

Harris, Lord 30–31
HM Inspectorate of Probation 98, 106, 130, 131–132, 134
HM Prisons and Probation Service (HMPPS) 51, 149
hospitals, and PbR 112–114
hostels, probation 135
House of Lords debates 18, 23, 30, 55–56, 94
House of Commons Debates 146
Howard, Michael 36–38

Institute of Probation 90; Chapter 6 passim
IT systems 100, 120

Khan, Sadiq 130

Labour Government 38, 46
legitimacy of rules 161–162, 173–174
Lidington, David 61, 117–118

Magistrates Association 8
management of probation service; see also NOMS 49–50
managerialism 31, 35, 39, 49–50
markets and privatisation 105
Marx, Karl, and probation training 75
Maude, Francis 8
Mayoral model, of governance 152–153
McNally, Lord 55–56
mechanical reporting 156
mentoring of offenders 135–137, 163

National Association of Probation Officers (NAPO) 17–18, 69–71, 89, 93, 99, 146
National Association of Senior Probation Officers 30
National Audit Office 99, 108, 109 114, 121 133
National Offender Management Service (NOMS) 51–52, 53, 68, 83–84, 93, 154
National Probation Service (NPS) 3, 23, 31, 43, 53, 55; passim 79, 90; governance of 148–154
National Standards 78, 147, 157
neo liberal ideal 8–14, 36, 90, 105, 172
nothing works 27–28, 40–42

offenders, characteristics of 131
offender's views, on probation 133–134
Offender Management Act 47, 53
Offender Rehabilitation Act (2007 and 2014) 53–54, 57, 79
Outsourcing of Electronic monitoring 35; see also privatisation

parole 81, 155, 159
partnerships, in probation 39
payback scheme 107
Payment by Results (PbR) 3, 13–14; Chapter 4 passim; dangers of,

creaming 115; gaming 115; parking 115; criminal justice, 116–117; errors in, 114; outcomes of 115
petition, against privatisation 15–16, 89
piloting, of privatisation 58, 88
Police and Crime Commissioners 152
Police Federation 35
Police National Computer 113
Prison Officers Association 13
prison, private 33, 63
"Prison Works" 37–38
Private Finance Initiative 1
Privatisation, of CRCs 12; of NPS, 12
privatisation, defined 11–12; in criminal justice 13; and neo liberal ideal 10–11; objections to 14–20; outsourcing 11–12
probation expenditure 37
probation ideal 5–6; see also ethos of
probation orders 7, 32, 43, 171, 173; and low level offenders, 50
Probation Trusts 57

Radzinowicz, Sir Leon 22
Rainor House 72
Ramsbotham, Lord 18, 56, 58, 94, 117, 144, 150–152, 170
reconviction rate, of ex prisoners 2
rehabilitation, under privatisation 103,104–105
Rehabilitative Activity Requirements 106
Reid, John 19, 83, 93
reports for the courts 4, 155, 164–170
resettlement prisons 127–128
resettlement services 127–130; see also Through The Gate
Risk Assessment Units 95
risk register, for legislation 58–60
risks, of reoffending 99

savings, on privatisation see costings
selection of probation officers 71–74

Seebohm Report 25–26
Selous, Andrew 2, 22
senior probation officers 49
service conditions, of CRCs 97–99; of NPS 97–99
sentencing of offenders, after privatisation 121
Stacey, Dame Glenys 120, 132, 147, 174; see also HM Inspectorate of Probation
Statement of National Objectives and Priorities (SNOP) 30–31, 63
Straw, Jack 34, 36, 47, 72
Strategic Risk Assessment 57–60
Strengthening probation, building confidence 20, 62
Stretfeild Committee Report 167–168
strike, of probation officers 89
social work, and probation 26, 71–74, 74–76
supervision of offenders 130, 154–170; of children 44–45

training, of probation officers 71–74
Transforming Rehabilitation 3, 22, 52, 53; passim 68, 87, 90, 153
Through The Gate Services 55, 119; Chapter 5 passim; 132–136, 137
Trusts, Probation 94

unpaid work see payback

victims, of crime 45
victims services for 45, 154
victim support 77–78
voluntary services 39, 137

Wales, probation services in 149
Wallace, Ethnie 68
'What Works' 37, 40–42
Wolds prison 63
Woolf, Lord 57, 130, 150
Wootton, Barbara 62–63